1968 and I'm Hitchhiking Through Europe

The Roman Forum

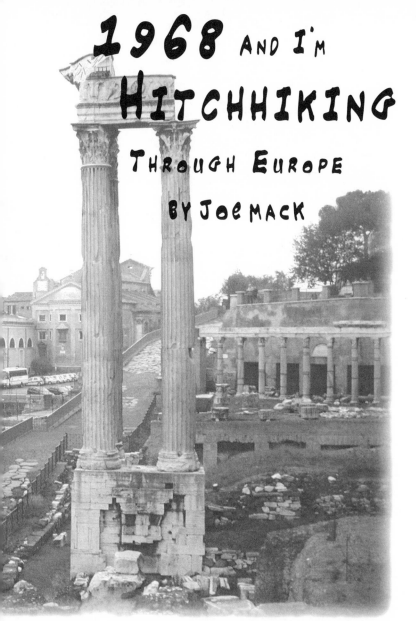

1968 AND I'M
HITCHHIKING
THROUGH EUROPE
BY JOE MACK

Solid Press Publishing

Library of Congress Control Number: 2005928945

PUBLISHER'S DATA

Mack, Joe
1968 and I'm Hitchhiking Through Europe/Joe Mack
First edition

ISBN 0-9769503-0-8

1.   Biography and Autobiography
2.   History
3.   Political Science
4.   Social Science
5.   Sports and recreation (hiking)
6.   Transportation
7. Travel
First person non-fiction narrative action-adventure

Printed in the United Sates of America
on recycled, acid-free paper

Solid Press Publishing
Philadelphia
http://www.solidpress.com

This book is dedicated to my
three children
And their many friends
Now grown up

It is time
To share the world I traveled

Table of Contents

CHAPTER 1

THE LAST WEEK BEGINS

The day begins as another cool, foggy, summer morning. After walking to the cloverleaf I simply turn around, face oncoming cars, and stick out my thumb. I need to be the next lucky guy. Without luck, I could easily be waiting many hours for my first ride of the day.

The city is Hamburg, Germany. Dozens of hitchhikers spread themselves along the entrance ramp to the main highway-leaving town. Cars are stopping frequently. Sometimes they stop so men can get out and pee on the bushes, but every few minutes a car stops to give someone a ride. Hitchhikers are also arriving frequently so the number of us waiting stays about the same.

Getting picked up is like winning a lottery. We are traveling for free, meeting other people, being invited into their cars and sometimes into their homes. This is the experience of a lifetime.

Around me there are teenaged, middle-aged, and elderly hitchhikers. I see a few "drop-out" hippies with dirty hair and dirty clothes, several young women, a man in a business suit, and some other people who look like they are waiting for rides to work. However, most hitchhikers look like I think I look, a young male college student wearing jeans and carrying a backpack and sleeping bag.

Some of us have our right arm out and thumb up; others have adopted the European auto-stop style (slowly moving the right arm up and down.) Everyone is waiting for the moment to arrive.

Drivers pull over next to someone (or a couple). They talk about mutual destinations and then into the car goes the hitchhiker. If the car stops halfway between two hitchhikers, the driver points at the beneficiary of his or her generosity. Not everyone speaks the same language here; all of us are just going in the same direction.

Today I want to make it to Copenhagen, Denmark. To be truthful, my aim is to catch up with two young Swedish girls who should be back home now. I met them in Venice. We had fun walking around the royal palace. I ran into them again in Vienna. We enjoyed the afternoon together in a museum and nearby park. We exchanged phone numbers, addresses, and made plans to link up in Prague, the capital of Czechoslovakia. We did.

They traveled by train. I hitchhiked and covered the distance in one day with the help of a dozen different drivers.

The two girls are cousins. The older one's name is Marie and the younger one calls herself Ice. They are nice and attractive in a Swedish sort of way. I got to know them better in Prague.

The last time I saw them was the night we raided the President's orchard (the orchard behind the house of the President of Czechoslovakia). It was late. There were four of us. We snuck down an alleyway right behind the President's residence, climbed over a fence and picked ripe fruit from his trees. Marie was hesitant. Ice was not.

Our folly lasted about two minutes. Then alarms started screaming and men rushed out from the house yelling something in Czech. The four of us ran out the alley and back to the main street.

Immediately a black Mercedes pulled up; plainclothes police jumped out and stopped us at the intersection. Other men ran up behind us. We were caught!

They do not read you your rights in communist Czechoslovakia. I stood there and wondered what they would do. Our fourth accomplice, a Czechoslovakian medical student who suggested the raid did not look upset. He whispered we had no reason to worry; police guarding the President were good men.

They had us surrounded. When we started to speak English among ourselves, the police started to talk among themselves. We waited minutes for them to do anything. More police arrived and walked up among us.

Our Czech student tried to placate them. Maybe it worked. Next to them, he looked very small. They talked quietly to him. He translated what they said.

They told him he was a bad influence on us, "the three foreign visitors." They said, "The streets are not safe for young girls late at night," and they lectured him.

Somehow, the police separated my Czech friend and me from the two Swedes without my noticing. A minute later, I saw Ice and Marie waving good-bye from over by the Mercedes. They did not look upset. The police told us they were going to take them back to their hotel.

When the car rolled away with the girls inside the driver yelled something at us. The Czech student said, "He yelled next time, they would arrest both of us for disturbing the public order and we should go home now unless we want to go to jail."

I turned around. My friend and I were the only people around; all the other men had vanished. The cobblestone intersection was quiet again. We got off lightly I thought, and I hoped the two Swedes only got a free ride home.

The next morning the Czech student told me he had talked to the girls on the phone. They were fine. He said they had already left for the airport to catch the plane to Sweden.

I knew this was supposed to be their plan but I regretted not saying good-bye, and not asking them about their police escort home. Ever since Strasbourg, France I have been aiming to see them again and hear their story directly.

Strasbourg is where a friendly couple I met in Germany lives. They invited me to visit and promised me a blind date. The date did not go well. Later, I talked to them about Ice and Marie and they encouraged my desires.

At that point, I was slowly hitchhiking towards Amsterdam; I decided to travel to Sweden instead.

My flight home is leaving in one week. Well,

admittedly, I could be calling the girls on the phone but talking to Ice and Marie from hundreds of miles away is not what I want. Seeing them again is on my mind.

So now I have told you why I am hitchhiking on this particular highway today and why I need just one driver to stop for me, any one driver.

A car is pulling over next to me. My good luck is returning. Yes! My first ride is happening early, long before the sun gets hot.

A U.S. soldier stationed in Germany picks me. He is the first American to give me a ride all summer. His name is Bob and he has just begun a two-week leave. He says he wants to see Europe. He was going to drive around all by himself but now he has picked me up instead.

Bob and I have come here from two very different worlds. He just left the barracks and army life. I have been as free as a bird all summer. I tell him about having nothing better to do than spend my last week of freedom traveling north to see the Swedish girls again.

Bob is sympathetic to my quest. He will drive me all the way to Sweden.

Northern Germany looks like New Jersey; the autobahn looks like the Jersey turnpike. One difference is cars here drive very, very fast.

In Germany a few days ago, a man treated me to how the finest model Mercedes rides at 140 MPH. It rides very smoothly. It seems to float above the road. Maybe we were floating. I noticed the driver never touched the brake pedal and had a loose grip on the steering wheel. I think he was not really steering the car. He just kept pointing it straight ahead.

This big, rough looking, middle-aged German guy and I were flying up the autobahn and he started telling me his life story. He was a patriotic teenager during World War 2. Then his invincible Germany surrendered unconditionally. His world shut down. At night, the lights didn't come on because there was no electricity. When he turned the sink handle, no water ran from the tap. Stores had no food to sell. His family had money but that didn't matter. Everyone was always hungry. Almost everyone he knew got sick.

U.S. soldiers saved their lives. He began to see them everyday and they did not act like conquerors. They respected ordinary Germans. Working for Americans he earned food, money, and later wealth as a contractor. This was how he could afford the most expensive cars in the world.

He said, "I love America and Americans." This was why he stopped for me. (And he wanted to tell me his story.) But he kept the speedometer at a steady 140 MPH and took his eyes off the road too many times. As in all other cars, this car had no seatbelts to wear. (Like that would matter.)

Then he turned, looked at me and said, "My American Oldsmobile Super 88 is a much better car than this Mercedes."

My dad owns an Oldsmobile Super 88. This Mercedes is a much better car. I asked if I heard him right. He repeated his claim without qualification. I did not disagree. Distracting him further would be a bad idea. Every one and a half seconds we were traveling the length of a football field. One thousand and one, one thousand.

Bob is driving a practically new, yellow, Volkswagen Karmen Ghia sports car. This will not be one of those 140MPH trips however. The Karmen Ghia looks like a fast car but it only looks like a fast car. And this one was built for English Roads with the steering wheel on the right side. I am sitting in the "normal" driver's seat.

As I watch, landscapes go by. I try to talk to Bob. He says he has not thought about the Vietnam War. Then he says he is glad to be stationed in Europe instead. When I ask him, he tells me he will do whatever the army wants him to do. He never asks questions. End of subject.

It takes two to have a conversation and Bob will not even talk about girls more than, "There are no women in the army." He does not ask me any questions either.

I was taught asking questions and listening to answers show you are interested in the other person. You become interesting too. (And asking the right question might keep you out of trouble.) Here, my questions fail. Except for the changing scenery, it is a boring morning.

After driving a few hours from Hamburg, we arrive at a port and park on a pier. Germany and Denmark share a common border but Copenhagen is on an island. To get there we have to venture across the sea in a ferry.

The pier is crowded with a hundred other vehicles. Not just cars, I see double tractor-trailers and a long passenger train.

A man in a conductor's uniform comes over to our window and we buy tickets from him. I ask about the train; he says it is not waiting to discharge and pick-up passengers. Everything we see is going into the ship. The voyage is going to take several hours. People have to leave their vehicles, go upstairs and hang out in the casino, one of the restaurants, the movie theatre, or walk around the deck.

A huge, glistening, beautiful ocean-going vessel pulls up to the pier and we all drive in. Over the loudspeakers they tell us again, everyone must stay away from their vehicles. Passengers can even rent a cabin and sleep. Bob goes to a restaurant. I explore the ship.

Next thing I feel is the body of a young woman. And I see a full head of the reddest hair imaginable. I bumped into her hard. Or maybe since she was running down the stairs she rammed me. Doesn't matter. She sits down from the impact. I sit down next to her. I tell her I'm sorry.

She's OK. She's Norwegian. And she speaks English as if it were her native tongue.

She says her name but it escapes me. She is returning home. After graduating college in May and hitchhiking all summer she will be starting her new job as an elementary schoolteacher in her small Norwegian town.

I ask her, "Where did you hitchhike?"

She replies, "All around North Africa."

Sitting close together in the stairwell, sharing stories about traveling, makes time fly. She talks about going it alone in Morocco and Tunisia. She says the North African people were respectful of her and incredibly friendly. The most exciting places she visited were the cities of Casablanca and Tangiers (opposite the rock of Gibraltar). She loved the trip.

However, she was not planning to do it again. She did have serious "difficulties" in Southern France and again in Spain. Right now she needs to ditch her ride north and asks, "Can I travel with you?"

I say, "YES." She says she needs to hide in our car until it is time to go. I forget all about what the officials told us twice. I leave to find Bob and ask for the keys.

I find Bob. He asks if the Norwegian might be smuggling drugs.

"She's a schoolteacher," I tell him.

Bob says, "OK." He starts giving me the keys and then realizes the car is unlocked. I can just show her where it is and she can get in.

She looks scared in that stairwell when I return. We sneak downstairs and she hides in the back of Bob's car with a blanket over her. I leave thinking, "Am I a lucky guy or what?"

Now I am walking around the ship and seeing guy after guy who appears to be looking for someone. In my head, I am imagining every possible variation of what she might be running away from: an abusive boyfriend, unpaid debts, a white slavery gang.

If he (they) catch us, would we be in trouble? After all that has happened to me this summer, I have begun to believe I have some kind of defense against harm. I can deal with any scenario. Besides, she was totally convincing as a teller of the truth. She is just ditching her ride.

I am excited again. Adventure with a young woman who has so much confidence is exhilarating.

The ferry hits the dock and everyone walks down the stairs to their vehicles. Bob and I sit in his Karmen Ghia and then drive off the ferry. It is that easy. We are in Denmark, accelerating up the highway to Copenhagen.

I introduce the redhead to Bob as my Norwegian friend. She says her name again. I cannot even guess what letter of the alphabet it starts with. It ties my tongue. My problem with her name would be embarrassing except she says she is used to it. When I want her attention, I can just touch her shoulder. She has a freckled face, a strong athletic body, and a beautiful shoulder.

She, in this tiny car with us produces a euphoria that is a wonderful thing to experience. Bob listens while we tell travel stories.

At this point in my trip, I am telling everybody about my problems with police. Like at the end of my very first hitchhiking ride, when Generalissimo Franco's border guards detained us. The ride itself was really ugly, dangerous, and scary. I start by telling them about the crazy driver who picked us up.

Bob interrupts and asks what was said when the bad ride ended. I realize I remember it well enough to use quotation marks. I will never forget it.

I tell them, "I couldn't see. The car stopped. I yelled, 'Let's get out!' and my friend shouted back, 'NO. They have guns, don't move.'"

I finish the story. They like all my stories about trouble with authority.

She asks if I am one of those American student rioters Europeans read about.

Different college, I tell her.

She is thinking I go to Columbia University. In April, New York City police arrested over seven hundred students who occupied five school buildings there.

The students wanted to stop their school from building a gymnasium on land in a nearby public park. They also connected the Vietnam War to Columbia's research arm, the Institute for Defense Analysis. The students wanted to end the clandestine work the IDA was doing on their campus.

Columbia University officials liked things the way they were and would not compromise.

The occupation of the buildings lasted seven days. The eviction of the students was brutal. The riot made news around the world. My friends and I followed events there very closely.

The students did not riot.

After police violently evicted students in the fifth building, they turned around and charged into the large crowd watching the action. Many of the most serious injuries occurred then, after people occupying the buildings were arrested and taken away.

When police swinging nightsticks charged the bystanders, even conservative students who had been protesting the protestors were injured.

The police rioted.

I tell Bob and the Norwegian I had been in that kind of riot. It happened the night thousands of exuberant students paraded around my campus. We were celebrating because our school won the basketball championship.

A few people started rocking buses back and forth. Other students calmed the crowd and we continued our victory march.

The police stood by and did nothing until approximately one hundred students remained. We were standing on a walkway singing the school fight song. Then I saw two large vans pull up.

I was right there when dozens of helmeted police came out, formed a line and charged. They were swinging their nightsticks hard.

Bob and the Norwegian both want to know what happened to me. I tell them I had been standing in the front and center, but after the riot squad lined up and faced us I moved to the side and became a witness to everything that happened.

Those policemen started screaming as they charged. They plowed into the center of the crowd. I saw students turn and start running away but into each other, tripping, falling down. I watched the police clubbing students on the ground, police chasing people down the street, police hitting and hitting a few guys again and again with their nightsticks.

At the end I saw police walking back to their vans laughing, students walking in the direction of the university hospital holding their bleeding heads, and lots of young men and women crying.

For a while after the riot I became a "crazie." I think I was feeling guilty about avoiding the fight and angry no one was brought to justice for the brutality I witnessed. I hung out with other guys who were angry, cursed everything, and hated all rules.

I am lucky that did not last. Those students argued about what to do with anybody else who had an opinion. They never listened and just wanted to fight against authority.

Throughout history, young people have always been pushing the limits with their passions and idealism, and suffering the consequences or reaping the rewards. They are the group reacting to events first, trying new behaviors, and doing things their parents would never allow if parents could stop them.

Like traveling alone in North Africa.

The Norwegian says she did not know she had it in her. The people in the little fishing town where she grew up will be surprised she did it. When she left home, she actually had no particular destination. The trip just happened.

She hitchhiked south without a plan and trusted the kindness of strangers. {The author is putting in a word of caution here. I am not encouraging anyone, male or female, to do this.}

After traveling through Spain, she took a ferry to Morocco. She was welcomed into the homes of many North Africans. They fed her and she stayed with families without payment. She was never harassed. Wherever she went, she found courteous and kind people.

Everything worked out better than anyone could have foretold. Now she is returning home a stronger person then when she left.

From her bag, she pulls out a few of the treasures she is taking home: carved stone figures, beautiful scarves, silver rings, and a wooden hash pipe. But the hashish-"All gone."

Well, maybe on the ship I was technically correct about no drugs. However, the smell of hashish resin leaps out of that pipe and into my nose. It is potent without being loaded. It only needs to be lit up. I am the one always prepared with matches.

We ask Bob. He says, "I don't want any but it's OK with me if you guys light it up."

We do. Soon, laughter joins the three of us. Tears too. Bob is stoned from the smoke in the car. He blurts out how much he admires our spirit of adventure. He is 21 years old and has done nothing but hide his entire life. If he hadn't been drafted, he would still be living with his mom.

"God, I am still a virgin," he cries. Then he laughs too.

Rhythmic, pulsating, Arabic music is coming from Bob's radio. The beat is moving my foot, then leg, then body like great rock and roll will do. The beautiful farms of Denmark are flying by at 60mph. The daylight is fading. The highway is bringing us closer to Copenhagen. I am feeling the warmth of more orange sunshine than any sunset ever offered before. I am living in a beautiful moment.

But it gets very dark very quickly. It gets cold. This suburb of Copenhagen is industrial. The road signs are in Danish. None of us knows where to go. My drug high changes to anxiety. The Norwegian says she is exhausted. Bob says he is starving. We put him in charge.

Soon on the roadside we see a Chinese restaurant, and next-door, a modern, nice looking motel. Two great finds! And just in time.

Bob pulls into the parking lot of the motel. He tells us to register for a room and says he will go next door and buy everyone something to eat and drink. He also says we can spend the night here on him; we will split up tomorrow.

My Norwegian friend and I walk into the motel office. After showing our passports and signing a paper, we have no problem renting a room for tonight. The motel will even let us (Bob) pay in the morning.

The clerk escorts us to our room. He is unlocking the door. Suddenly, I am looking at the most luxurious motel room I have ever seen. The furniture is all new and Danish modern. I see plush carpeting, a small kitchenette, and paintings on the walls.

The three of us go inside. The room is nice and warm. It looks spotless, smells great, and has dark drapery. Near the door are a round coffee table and two cushioned armchairs. In the center, I see two beds.

The clerk says he saw Bob get out of the car with us and he knows three of us are staying in this room tonight. He opens the closet, removes a cot, and carries it between the beds.

We say nothing. She and I just sit in the chairs and watch the clerk take his time setting up the cot. He keeps his eye on us. Then he leaves.

18

My Norwegian friend starts talking a mile a minute saying she is not the girl I think she is and that she left her ride on the ferry because he was pressing her for sex but she was not going to give it to him because she didn't like him at all and she is apologizing to me about asking a stranger for a big favor and is saying I just looked like a guy she could trust and I am hearing about the "difficulties" in Spain and Southern France when drivers attempted to rape her and she dissuaded one but the other hurt her and she knocked the guy out because she knows karate.

I tell her I am just having fun and trying not to hurt anyone.

Now she is standing up and showing me her black and blue arm, and showing me her muscles; she has big muscles. She is punching out some karate moves and throwing a kick up into the air.

We are still stoned. I am very stoned. I wait outside to make sure Bob can find the room.

Eventually Bob arrives with two bags of fantastic smelling Chinese food, plus beer, vodka, and soda. He apologizes profusely about not asking us what to get and for taking such a long time. "I stood there forever deciding what to order," he says. We quickly gobble up the food. I drink two beers.

We're all tired. I haven't felt strong for days. I haven't slept well all week. I haven't eaten right all summer. We could go to bed now. We draw straws; she gets the cot between Bob and me.

I need to take a shower but am feeling lightheaded. She grabs her backpack, says she will take a quick one and heads for the bathroom. Bob opens the vodka and starts drinking it. He and I say nothing to one another.

She returns in flannel pajamas with her hair up in a towel. Bob and I are already lying down. For me, the room is spinning a bit. She turns out the lights. I reach out to touch her shoulder and say good night. I don't know what I touched; it was soft. The room spins much faster.

She gives out a yelp and whispers something that sounds like "not now." My mind goes on overload. It is actually fuzzing up. All I can think to say is "I was only trying to touch your shoulder and say good night."

Bob laughs. In the dark room, she lifts herself up and takes my hand. I go to roll over but I cannot roll over. I can't even move. For me the night ends now.

Next thing I know is waking up in the morning. They are already up. Even before they say anything to me, I am REALLY ANGRY with myself. Being exhausted and drinking too much, drinking and drugs, they are BAD IDEAS. When will I ever learn!

I don't have a hangover so that isn't the problem. It is the stupidity reverses good luck thing. I look at Bob. I could have been smiling this morning like Bob is smiling.

According to his account, after I passed out I began to snore very strangely and they could not get me to wake up.

I am still lying on the bed. My Norwegian friend is leaning over close to me and saying, "I was worried about you but Bob said he wasn't worried; he slept in an army barracks every night with guys who snored like you."

Last night, they rolled me over and I just changed my tune. Then they began to laugh. Neither is mad at me for snoring. It re-energized them.

She says, "There is a nightclub across the street and we walked over to it. Bob can dance!" She had fun. They came back, slept a little, and went out for breakfast. They even brought me back a cup of coffee.

Both look good. Bob's smile is big. He is smiling from ear to ear.

Now Bob says he wants to get going; if I want a ride into downtown Copenhagen, I have to get out of bed this minute. He won't even give me ten minutes to take a shower. I get up. The three of us leave the motel together.

The ending is her leaning out the car's window, saying good-bye and how I shouldn't worry about her; Bob is very nice and he is going to drive her all the way home to Norway. She says they would have invited me along but the back seat of the Karmen Ghia is awful.

Bob just waves goodbye. They drive away.

I turn around. He's dropped me off in the Porno Zone. How long will it be until I feel lucky again?

CHAPTER 2

FIRST RIDE – ALMOST THE LAST RIDE

This morning Copenhagen isn't warm, not even close. It feels more like November than August. The city is socked in by a cloud at street level; visibility extends to the other side of the street. I'm beginning to feel the mist on my face. I, like you, avoid getting wet, and shivering with cold.

Now the water in the air is penetrating my light jacket. I'm on some corner in a city I never planned on visiting. I'm waiting for purpose to re-occur to me. I'm wet, shivering, and feeling even colder.

Under a theater marquee, I find some shelter and see an advertisement for the movie. The words are in Danish but the photos do not need any translation. The big blow-up shows beautiful bare-breasted women dancing in an 18th Century palace. Men are dancing with them wearing 18th Century costumes. This is a soft-core porno flick in color with a big cast and historical theme.

You can't see movies like this in the U.S. Bare breasts are obscene onscreen. They might get the Hollywood director banned or the theater owner arrested.

America has Blue Movies. They are low budget, poorly filmed, and graphic. Men see them at private clubs and college frat parties. I know because I was exposed to them there. I saw men laugh and heard them ridicule the women. Blue movies make sex look cheap and treat women like trash. Those guys might be comfortable with that, but not me.

The theater is opening for the first show of the day. The women in the advertisement look beautiful, even healthy. Middle-aged men in raincoats walk by me, going inside.

Suddenly, I do not want anyone seeing me at this place. My reaction strikes me as funny because I am anonymous in Copenhagen; no one I know will see me here.

I like the idea of seeing naked female bodies but not on film. I walk back into the cold rain and away from the theater. My canvas poncho goes on. The last time I actually wore this poncho was while walking across the Pyrenees Mountains in Spain. That was a warm rain on a hot summer day during the first week I was in Europe.

The story immediately comes to mind. It was after our days in Pamplona, after our mornings trying to catch the bulls.

I was still traveling with my college roommate, Jim. We had landed in Paris and planned to hitchhike the entire summer as a pair. But that was the last day we traveled together. And for many reasons, it was the longest day of the entire trip. I will never forget any part of it.

We went to Pamplona for excitement. We wanted to be at the running of the bulls. Thousands of other people also wanted to be there. Most of them were Spanish men wearing white shirts, white pants, and red scarves. Jim and I spent three days in Pamplona and constantly saw local people wandering around drinking Spanish wine.

At night, many of these same people were lying on the ground in parks, alleys and streets. They were either asleep or passed out. Jim and I were drinking too but I have known him for three years and he never drank that much. Good for him. And his habit was good for me too.

On our second night we walked in the direction of loud music. We joined a group of inebriated local men who were slowly walking in the same direction. We all arrived at a big festival in a small, European town square.

We discovered a scene with hundreds of Spanish men and many visitors drinking and tightly holding on to one another, snake dancing in long lines like Conga dancers. And we saw hundreds of other people drinking and watching them. I am trying to describe a courtyard where a thousand people were touching one another, drinking, staring, pushing, dancing, swearing, partying, vomiting and passing out like there was no tomorrow. This wasn't like some wild fraternity party; it was worse.

It was very physical like a bad football game. There was too much released anger and people weren't playing. They were banging into one another, trading stares and insults, and threatening one another. I saw punches traded between two groups of men. I heard people whispering about seeing an ugly fistfight. We were caught up in this.

The crowd pushed us past a college-age American man leaning against a stone column holding a bloody handkerchief on his face and a wine bottle in his other hand. Several American women were crying to us. Men in the crowd had groped them, hurt them.

The Spanish police, called the Guardia Civil, were there in force. What could they do? Some policemen looked scared themselves, others menacing. Most wore big, black, bright shiny plastic hats, almost like Napoleon's hat. But the police did not look funny. They walked in pairs and every one of them carried a machine gun.

An American stopped us and said he just witnessed the police strike a rifle butt into the face of a white-shirted local. He said, "It was not like in the movies. The man collapsed straight down real quick. He didn't fall backwards. He didn't get up." The American suggested it was time to leave.

But the crowd was so tight, as it moved around, Jim and I moved apart. I scanned the crowd but couldn't see him. I saw police looking nervous. I saw some had their fingers on the triggers of their weapons. I was very tense.

It is 1968. Thirty years ago, the army of Generalissimo Francisco Franco was fighting to overthrow the Spanish Republic. The general had promised his soldiers a quick victory over the governing coalition of Republicans, Socialists, Communists, and powerful Anarchist Collectives.

Franco promised his soldiers they would be heroes for uniting the country. The men believed him. They followed his orders, fought a bloody three-year long civil war against the Spanish Republic, and devastated their own country. I saw what Franco's victory gave the Spanish people during my train ride to Pamplona.

(Jim and I did not hitchhike to the festival in Pamplona. We traveled there from Paris by rail because of what we had heard. Hitchhikers can spend days trying to get out of Paris. They can go round and round on the highways that circle the city. At night, hitchhikers might have to sleep in a field or behind a gas station. For a meal, they might have to walk miles to a restaurant or eat nothing. Someone we knew waited all afternoon to get a ride and it went only a few miles. He gave up hitchhiking before he really got started. We did not want a bad start to our hitchhiking adventure. Besides, Parisians intimidated us. We took the train to Spain two days after we arrived.)

Our train stopped at the French-Spanish border and every passenger had to get off. Outside, the sun felt much closer to my skin than it had ever felt before. It was still morning but the temperature was over 100 degrees in the shade. The air was stagnant and taking a deep breath burned my lungs.

Most of us were tourists but there were also some very wealthy Spanish women who had been on a shopping trip to Paris and several Spanish businessmen. Everyone had to wait outside and began to complain about the oppressive heat. After a few minutes, we went into the customs house and had our passports stamped. Then we walked out to see a different train on the tracks.

For us, the Spanish railroad authority brought in beautiful dark blue, railroad passenger cars. Their shiny clean exteriors glistened in the sun and we all climbed inside.

Some people complained about having to climb up the steps but the air-conditioned comfort shocked and refreshed everyone. We sat in leather armchairs around wooden coffee tables. Plush beige carpeting softened the floor. Smartly uniformed waiters offered us food and drink. Jim and I were not hungry or thirsty. We declined.

The interior looked new but was not. Only a trained crew of workers could do that kind of vacuuming, dusting, and polishing. They even washed the windows so perfectly every passenger viewed the sizzling hot railroad yard like there was no glass.

This train was beyond first class. I sat among other students with backpacks and bedrolls but felt like a rich American, rubbing elbows with wealthy travelers from around the world.

After traveling one hundred yards into Spain, the luxury train came to a halt. A train carrying local people was rolling by right next to ours.

A well-dressed Spanish woman near us exclaimed, "Don't look!" Some people hurriedly pulled down their window shades. But college students are not children; no one tells us not to look. Our window shades stayed up.

Suddenly, we all learned an entirely different world was out there. Cattle cars containing men moved very slowly past our brilliantly clear windows.

One at a time we saw each man. They had bronze skin and dark hair. Their ages ranged from sixteen to sixty. Every man was thin; most were wearing white shirts, white pants, and red scarves. We saw a few sitting on dirty floors, most standing at open doors; some were hanging off the cattle car sides. There were no chairs, benches, or seats.

The local men saw these glistening dark blue passenger cars standing right next to them. A few swung themselves out and reached for us.

What rolled by us for several minutes was public transport as I imagined might exist in crowded, poverty stricken Asia, or Africa. Actually, it was much worse than I imagined. I could see straw and manure on the floor of the cattle cars. The Spanish railroad authority had not even bothered to have a crew sweep out the cars for the locals. That was why most men traveled standing up. There were even men sitting on the roofs.

The students were commenting on what we all saw. I said our government wouldn't allow Americans to be treated like cattle. Protests would happen; politicians would be voted out. Our government is of the people, by the people, and for the people.

In a dictatorship, government is of, by, and for the people who own it. Other people have no rights that can't be taken away. Protesting is wrong. I heard what the Spanish government did in May when students peacefully protested in Madrid. It published a warning in the newspapers. It said if you attended a meeting that turned into a forum for subversive opinions, you would be subject to arrest and trial. (Franco had spies everywhere.)

In 1968, young people around the world were loudly expressing their opinions. Demonstrations for student power, peace, and justice were happening in countries ruled by dictators and in countries where people thought the police protected the right to protest. I saw protests on TV, read about them in newspapers, and went to some myself. Of course, most students never went to a demonstration and the parents of many protestors were appalled at their children's behavior.

On the train, the Spanish conductor disapproved. He gave us a very dirty look and pulled down every shade. He twisted their latches and shut them securely. All the students went silent. We split up. More minutes went by.

Our train moved forward, stopped again and we felt the bang of the cattle car train hooking up to the back of our luxury train. For two hours, rich and poor stayed united and we all traveled to Pamplona together.

The two different trains helped explain the tense atmosphere at the festival. In the old town square, I was seeing the same men I saw riding cattle cars. Except now they were drunk. To them every American in Pamplona was a rich American. And Spain was a poor country. That morning I had seen third world living conditions for some Spanish citizens.

If the people protested, they were risking their lives. The Spanish police did not carry nightsticks. They had machine guns. At the festival in Pamplona, if police were provoked, what would they do? Would they spray the crowd with bullets?

That night, I heard a drunk American complaining loudly about feeling hostility from the locals when he tried to buy a beer at a tavern. And when the man standing next to me told him, "You're lucky they didn't slice your face," I realized more violence was a definite possibility.

It was time to leave so I was glad to see Jim in the crowd. We decided to go back to the apartment where we had already paid to spend the night. We had slept on the floor there the previous night.

As we walked back, we passed by other partygoers passed out on the sidewalk, in the gutter, and down alleys. We made it to the apartment without incident. We slept without a problem in our sleeping bags on the floor.

In the morning, the couple who turned their apartment into a youth hostel woke everyone at dawn. We rushed out to see the bulls.

Did we join the race? We didn't get the chance. We were following behind the bulls. We were trying to catch up to them. They were always several blocks ahead of us. We followed the crowd and the bulls to the early morning mayhem in the Pamplona arena.

We bought tickets and went inside the stadium, up into the stands, and watched an amazing scene unfold. About fifty men and at least six bulls were in the bullring together.

We saw what you expect of angry bulls, and of men with more guts than brains. As bulls ran near them, men were reaching out and trying to touch the animals. Some men were succeeding, recoiling, falling down, and/or being pushed around by the bulls. All the men were banging into each other, tripping, standing dead still or running away as the bulls ran through the group again and again.

I was thinking the men were showing off and the bulls were having fun. Actually, I was watching fewer and fewer men facing the bulls.

The bulls were clearing the ring of men, butting at them with their capped horns, chasing them down, and even stepping on some. They were forcing men to hide behind barriers, and making some jump over a wooden wall. Bulls were also leaving the arena, running out a nearby gate.

Soon, the action slowed down. The last few bulls were facing the last few idiots. Some men were wearing modern western clothing and others wore the white uniforms of the local people. If any one man ran too far from the barriers the bulls chased him back or tried to knock him down. A few men were lying on the ground, not moving. There was blood on the sand. The blood of men, not bulls.

Groups of men were running out from behind the barriers, being heroes, grabbing and pulling victims of trampling to safety behind the barriers. If you had broken ribs, being tugged like that would cause excruciating pain.

At the end of amateur hour, all the men were out of the arena and a couple of very large, black bulls controlled the ground. The crowd cheered mightily. The bulls left. Other men cleared the ground of hats, shoes, and shirts. We waited in the hot sun.

Then the matadors strutted out and the bullfight began. Jim and I left when the score reached a predictable Matadors 3 Bulls 0. We had enough of living in a country filled with hardship, anger and violence. Our thoughts turned to hitchhiking out of Spain.

We bought some bread and fruit at a market and walked to the north edge of town. The road to France was a narrow, black, macadam strip shimmering between two big fields of green vegetables. Visible on the distant horizon and covered with a purple haze, I saw the Pyrenees mountain range.

The morning had many hours left but the heat was already burning through our shirts. We stuck out our thumbs. Without any trouble at all, we got a white, two-door coupe to stop for us.

It was exciting; here was the first ride of our hitchhiking adventure!

Trouble started now.

We ran up to a driver who was yelling something at us. And to our surprise, two other Americans were already in the small car. They were protesting the car stopping for us. He was vigorously motioning at them to move over and for us to get in. They moved over; we got in.

Despite four years of high school Spanish, I didn't understand a single word the driver was yelling.

Squashed inside this car built for two adults and three small kids were five men and all their stuff. Our driver popped the clutch and took off. We headed towards the Pyrenees and France.

The man was driving way too fast, swerving around corners, and using the gears for braking. I was sitting in the back seat being tossed around and tossed into the guy next to me whose name I never learned. Too often, the driver twisted around and started yelling at us. What were his reasons?

The four of us were whispering about getting out, but how? The car never stopped.

He was driving like a maniac. We zoomed into a village with no traffic lights. Straight ahead was a dead end. He did not slow down. A huge truck nearly turned into us. Our driver drove onto the sidewalk and veered to the right, down the street the truck came from. I saw it all out the windshield. It was not funny, like on TV.

The driver was not stopping for anything and he was spending more and more time screaming. At who? Who knows?

Off and on, one of the hitchhikers I didn't know was yelling back in Spanish. It didn't matter. Our driver probably was a Basque. That was why I couldn't understand him. He was not speaking Spanish.

Millions of people in Northern Spain are

Basques first, Spaniards second. There are other Basques who just hate Spain.

These Basques won't learn Spanish. They fought the Spanish government long before Franco; they fought against Franco; they are still fighting. Some Basques are still killing people today to proclaim their independence from Spain.

I had a bad thought. It was dawning on me, on us. Our sweating, yelling, crazed driver was one of them.

Next, we were climbing up a mountain. His car was slowing down. Someone suggested jumping out. I was willing to lose my backpack and sleeping bag. But the American at the front door wasn't ready to jump out of a moving car. He would do it when we stopped.

Next, the driver was spinning us around hairpin turns. We were crying out loud. It was hot in the car. Our tears did not last. We turned onto a dirt road. The distance from Pamplona to France is only about 25 miles. The border was close, said my map. But no dirt road's on it, "NO DIRT ROAD!"

We were going to cross into France using this dirt road. He was still driving like a maniac.

It would take too long for the four of us to jump out. Jumping out was stupid. He never stopped and he was still yelling.

We discussed fighting him to turn off the car.

We might hit a tree or turn over into the ditch. It could kill us all. But if we didn't do something, we might all die anyway. Or we might end up in France.

Someone said, "Grab the keys." That was another idea that sounded better from the back seat. He was still cursing. He was going to keep driving.

For my safety, I slipped down behind the front seat, curled up, and waited. A few seconds went by. The car stopped. Everyone was quiet. I yelled, "Let's get out!"

"NO. They have guns, don't move," Jim shouted back.

"What!" I didn't believe him.

Slowly I lifted my head and saw soldiers with machine guns surrounding us. They were pointing them at us through the windows, inches from our faces. Our driver had stopped yelling and started crying. The soldiers began yelling at us.

They took the driver out first and he disappeared into the building next to us.

Next, the soldiers were turning their attention to us. We raised our passports. They must have been wondering, "What the hell are four Americans doing in that car with this guy?" It took them too long, at least an hour to find out. They interrogated each one of us separately.

One at a time, they took us out of the car and

into the building. I could see it was an old border outpost, a small one story, one room building with brown stucco walls outside and brown stucco walls and a dirt floor inside. The wind, dust, and even rain could come in the windows because the windows had no glass.

They interrogated the three other Americans first. I heard everything. I learned these soldiers did not speak English. I learned none of us should speak Spanish, not a word.

We were unable to answer their questions. There was only so far an interrogation like that could go before it crossed over the line. They were hostile and loud. They searched our gear but they had not hurt any of us (so far.)

My turn; they brought me inside. The hot, humid air smelled of sweat and fear. Sunbeams flooded the room. Dust danced in the light. Everything was a shade of brown. They took me to a chair and I sat down.

The soldiers rolled out my sleeping bag on a big old wooden table. They squeezed it. They examined it closely. Then they opened my backpack and spread out all my possessions on top of the bag. I carried mostly clothes, snacks, and maps. They said nothing to me.

An officer came in and took charge. He looked

at everything. He poked a pack of my condoms with his stick and said something. The soldiers did not smile. I worried.

The officer became upset. He shook the book, "Nigger" by Dick Gregory, taken from Jim's backpack, in my face. I have no idea why. The book is an autobiography of a black comedian turned social activist. It opened some eyes to racial discrimination in the North, not just in the Deep South.

Even if I could have translated what he was yelling at me, I would not answer him. Different languages can make communication impossible. This was the one time so far when that was good.

They brought Jim back in. They returned his book and backpack. I repacked my gear. They sat us both on the bench and nothing happened for a while.

No one told us we could go but finally the men waved their guns in the direction of the door. I guessed that motion meant we could leave. Jim and I left. Things could have been so much worse; I was suddenly feeling elated.

Outside, we looked around. The two other Americans were nowhere around. We heard a man crying somewhere. It sounded like our driver. This whole day had been very surreal and I could see it was going to stay that way. What was next; call a cab?

The border outpost was in a high valley

surrounded by a forest and between two mountains. We saw a farmer's field in the distance with the sun on it. We had to walk out on the dirt road we came in on.

First, we had to walk past the only other building at the border outpost, a beat up old Jail, two stories high. It had bars on the windows and men looking out at us between the bars, calling out to us. More than one man was crying.

We aimed to get back to the main road and hitchhike to our original destination, a city on the coast of France named Biarritz. It's not far really, just five or ten miles. We had to hitchhike.

We turned positive. We assured each other we could make it there before nightfall. Even though we were off the map, we told each other we were glad to be alive, free, and to feel the sun shining on us.

Soon Jim and I re-joined the main road. We were walking up and down low, rolling mountains. These were really foothills, close to where the Pyrenees Mountain range meets the Atlantic Ocean. The road took us to a plateau and past rich farmland.

The area was beautiful but we needed food. Maybe an hour went by. Dark clouds moved in on the blue sky and then a steady rain began to fall.

Along the highway was a large tavern. In we went. The big female bartender spoke Spanish but could not, or would not serve us food. She offered no explanation or regret. Jim and I just ate the bread and fruit from our backpacks. Then I took off my wet shirt to the amusement of some old men who were watching. I put on a dry shirt. And I put on the poncho I'm wearing right now.

What a memory. I am getting wet in Copenhagen thinking about being wet in Spain.

The rain in Spain was a different rain. There it was warm. Here it's cold, and blowing horizontally into my face. There it was coming straight down, and it smelled different too, like farms, and earth and trees. Here the rain smells vaguely like the sea. There I was spending my last day with Jim and had no choice about what to do. Here I am alone and have only choices.

I choose to leave Copenhagen. I have only six days left before my plane leaves from Paris and I still want to see those two Swedish cousins again. I still have time; I know I can make it.

I walk to the waterfront and buy a ticket for the ferry to Malmo, Sweden. Ice, the younger one, lives about 200 miles North of Malmo in Gothenburg, Sweden. I have her phone number. Getting there will be easy. Other hitchhikers have told me they felt more welcome in Sweden than anywhere else in Europe. And I have had great luck with rides most everywhere else already.

Everywhere except the Spanish Pyrenees. Who was going to pick up two hitchhikers in the rain?

After the tavern, we walked three hours in the rain. My poncho covered my backpack, my bedroll and me. Jim had no poncho. He did not even bring along a raincoat. He and his stuff got soaking wet.

Very few cars passed us. There never was a road sign pointing in the direction of France, never a mileage marker with the distance to the border. In a dictatorship, knowledge, freedom, and travel are limited at the whim of the government. And it does no good to argue. We trusted our map.

One Spanish soldier after another stopped us as we walked. Each stood at a one-man guardhouse. There must have been a dozen of them between the tavern and the French border.

At first, I tried to explain what Jim and I were doing. This provoked questions and a search through our possessions by a guard who was bored, wet, and irritated at his post. Then I stopped any attempt to speak Spanish and we just showed them our passports. Doing this kept our delay to a minimum. We started walking downhill too. That was good for our legs and lifted our spirits.

As we walked out of the woods we met the end of the road and a small coastal town. Just as suddenly the rain stopped. The sun came out. Across the bridge was France. Instead of crossing over right away, we went into the first place we saw that advertised food.

Irun was the Spanish town's name. It was a small seaport with a fishing industry. The fleet was in.

Around the bar were many fishermen. A few of them were talking to one another. Some were smoking pipes and drinking beer. Most had their eyes fixed up on the black and white television set above the bar. "Daktari" was on.

These Spanish men were watching an American TV adventure show where white hunters drove their Land Rover around modern-day Africa. I never watched it at home. Here it was dubbed into Spanish and had a rapt audience.

After eating, Jim and I ran across that bridge. The next thing I did was cash one of my traveler's checks into French francs.

The sun was setting. Biarritz, our destination was the next town north. We started hitchhiking again and a car stopped quickly but it was a family with kids. Jim spoke French and told them the two of us would not fit. Another driver soon stopped for us and took us to the hotel district.

It turned out Biarritz was an expensive and popular resort. There were no cheap accommodations for students and the first two hotels we walked by had no vacancies.

1968 and I'm Hitchhiking Through Europe

We found a room but it cost us eight times what our budget was.

According to Jim, the desk clerk actually said he gave us the last vacant room in the hotel because he was a homosexual and thought we were homosexuals.

We paid a lot for a hot, seventh floor walk-up with only one small bed pushed under an angled, dormer roof. Even if we wanted to, both of us could not sleep in that bed. We flipped a coin; I slept on the floor.

In the morning, Jim announced we would split up. It was not because of what the desk clerk said but because of the car with kids in it. Rides would be easy to get alone, hard for two. He said it was the best option; his mind was made up.

I had not prepared for this. Jim was the one who did the research. Jim was the one with plans of what to see. And I told him so.

Jim told me the destinations were simple. Visit the capitals. Go to the great museums, parks, castles, ancient ruins, and palaces. I had a map. That's all I needed. He told me not to miss the Pantheon in Rome. He reminded me to avoid all the ring roads around large cities. (I did not need that advice again. I knew a hitchhiker could be stuck at one exit ramp after another and go in circles for a week.)

We agreed. Both of us would hitchhike separately across southern France, through Italy, and to Rome. Maybe we would run into each other along the way.

We walked to the highway leaving Biarritz, turned around, and stuck out our thumbs. Jim was behind me, then he was gone. I was alone.

Biarritz was such a long time ago, almost the entire summer.

Now the ferry to Malmo is leaving right away. I go aboard. It feels great to be going somewhere again. Going somewhere answers every question I have about what I'm doing.

CHAPTER 3

SETTING FOOT IN SWEDEN

Yesterday's ferry was big. Several restaurants, a movie theater, and a casino were on it. This ferry to Malmo is small. Exploring it is forbidden. Sitting in the passenger compartment is what I am supposed to do. The room is only the size of a school bus and the entrance is so low I am bending over to avoid hitting my head.

A young woman is moving over. Maybe it's so I can share the seat with her. Of course I'm sitting down next to her.

Sitting causes pain. Missing meals while hitchhiking has made me even thinner than I used to be. I'm so thin; my ass hurts from just sitting down on the hard wooden bench.

I never considered myself good looking. Now acne has re-appeared on my face. My college moustache has grown over my top lip. I have an uneven beard on my cheeks and chin. My shirt is wrinkled. My jeans need washing, and I definitely need a haircut. However, I understand the power of a smile. People smile back.

At this moment however, the young woman next to me does not smile back. She will not even look my way. I am at a loss for words to get her good attention. Maybe talk can wait.

My backpack and bedroll identify me as a certain kind of traveler. While sharing cafeteria tables or park benches some Europeans have ignored my presence. Others look at me and ask questions. Not just young people, all kinds of people want to know if I am a hitchhiker, where I have come from, and where I'm going.

People's curiosity has also provided me with many rides. Conversation has been easy if my driver speaks English.

On my first day hitchhiking alone in Southwestern France the drivers who picked me up were all local people going only a short distance. Most spoke at least a little English. Slowly I traveled from one town to another. My destination was five hundred miles away so five miles down the road was not very far. But I was in no hurry and everything I saw was interesting to me so short rides were fine.

In the beginning, it was good I was not stuck on a lonely intersection or on some traffic clogged cloverleaf for eight hours. I waited a half hour for one ride, an hour for the next; the cool morning became a beautiful sunny day.

The French roads had makes of cars on them I had never seen before. Directional arrows, road signs, and route numbers were plentiful and they matched up with the information on my map. I was in a changing landscape of farmlands, forests, river valleys, vineyards, and barren, parched earth.

The main road across France (north of Spain) did not pass by any towns; it went through the center of each one. The sidewalks and shops all had people going about their daily routine. Restaurants had people sitting at outdoor tables. Where each town ended farms or forests began. There were no suburbs, shopping malls, or super highways. There was just a paved road with one lane in each direction through woods and over hills from one place to the next.

I saw the French highway police several times. They slowed down and looked me over but they never got out of their cars.

In Germany, highway police actively checked the identification papers of hitchhikers. And at one autobahn on ramp, I saw them walk down an entire line of men and women checking everyone's ID. Then they got to me. They just looked at my passport and handed it back.

Not one driver stopped to pick up a hitchhiker during the half hour the German highway police inspected us.

When they got to the man who was standing closest to the autobahn, they put him in a police car and left with him. I thought about how this happens to hitchhikers in the U.S. too. However, it did not seem to happen in France.

On my first day hitchhiking, I smiled and waved at the police. One time a policeman waved back. I was having a good time hitchhiking alone.

One town had an old fortress along the street. In another town, a small palace had been renovated into a hotel. My lunch was at an outdoor café built about the time the Mayflower arrived at Plymouth Rock. Dinner was at a similar place. Hours later, a hundred miles further down the road, I started to wonder, where would I spend the night? I was well fed, warm, and filled with adventurous spirit. I had no reason to worry about hitchhiking at night. So I hitchhiked at night. It quickly became late.

Someone driving what looked like a tall Volkswagen Beetle stopped to give me a ride. He was a young Frenchman. His car was a Citroen not sold in the U.S. Inside were canvas seats like a director's chair might have. The car had a canvas sunroof and vinyl side windows. I saw no speedometer in the dashboard and no radio. This was a small, cheap car. I put my backpack and bedroll behind the front seat and squeezed myself inside. I will always be glad he stopped for me.

He said he would drive me almost to Narbonne on the Mediterranean, over two hundred miles away. He had a wedding to go to and needed to drive all night to get there. This Frenchman's English was limited but good enough to converse.

He pointed out landmarks. We drove past a town square that had a famous statue made by the artist, Pablo Picasso. And later we saw the huge, ancient, fortress-city of Carssone. Bright gold lights dramatically illuminated the tall, stone walls that had protected the city for centuries. The walls seemed ready to repel another invading army.

I felt every bump as if the Citroen had no suspension. A car with its headlights off came at us. It startled me. My driver pointed and said that car had no generator. Did he mean you could buy an even cheaper car than his? Was he saying you could buy a new car without an alternator so you had to drive with your lights off or your battery would die? Yes.

Why would anybody ever do such a crazy thing as drive at night with his or her headlights off?

As it got near midnight, I realized this man had picked up a hitchhiker to help him stay awake. Because he picked me up, I had to be that person.

I talked. But he only understood half of what I said. Talking was not working so well.

I used my hands a lot to tell him a good story about how anti-war demonstrators blocked the steps to the Pentagon, but this distracted him and he was driving fast on a skinny road in a dark forest. Distracting him was a bad idea.

I asked questions. He was a student. Our different languages were making this difficult. Time was dragging. I was not doing my job well. It was almost one A.M.

He began to sing. He sang loudly and very well. I applauded. He sang several French songs. Then he told me to sing.

I sang. I knew *Home on the Range*. That was bad. Then songs came back to me. I sang *Row, Row, Row your Boat* good enough to get him to sing the same tune with French lyrics. We sang Christmas songs, national anthems, some Beatle songs. Many songs came back to me.

I was suddenly glad for my good education. I went to a public school system where the taxpayers paid for music teachers in the schools. Then I recited some poetry I was required to memorize, and I did a fair job on Abraham Lincoln's *Gettysburg Address*. But it would have been better to give him that speech well and with passion.

It was maybe 2 A.M and we were dangerously tired. I turned toward the driver and put my right hand on the metal dashboard. He was singing a song with a strong rhythm and without warning, he hammered my hand with his fist. I was shocked.

I rocked backwards but was off balance. My hand fell back to the dashboard and he tried to hammer it again. I moved it and he hit the metal. I put it back and he sang and swung his fist down again.

Maybe it was a song about a man with a mallet. We sped though the forest singing and playing an automobile version of the whack-a-mole game. We were both laughing. We traveled down the bumpy road bouncing up and down like people in a horse and carriage. I swayed back and forth on the canvas seat as if I were sitting in a hammock.

Our car went off the pavement a couple of times. No other cars were on the road; at least we didn't hit any and we didn't hit any trees, or deer. Our game worked. We stayed awake. And alive.

It became way past the middle of the night. We were in the very dark hours long before dawn. Our singing had stopped. There were no other cars on the road. I was nodding off, asleep.

In Germany on the autobahn just last week, I had to grab the wheel as my driver fell asleep. I steered his Volkswagen over to the shoulder and he woke up.

My French driver was much younger, entirely sober, and he steered his Citroen off the road before he fell asleep. We slept for some time.

We both woke up when the sky started getting lighter. He just started driving again. We were in the mountains without any view of the eastern horizon so I never saw the sun come up. It quickly became morning.

Our car slowly climbed a steep incline and stopped at a town on a mountainside, at a fork in the road. He pointed east and said "Narbonne," pointed north and said "wedding," and repeated himself. It did not sound like an invitation but a goodbye.

I thanked him; he thanked me and we said goodbye. I got out. He dove away and I sat down at an outdoor table of a still closed café. It was so early in the morning the town looked deserted. I put my head down and fell sound asleep. I woke up to the café noise and bright sunshine.

And I jerk, and wake up on the boat to Malmo. Exhaustion is a frequent companion of hitchhikers. The rhythmic rocking of our voyage across the narrows between Denmark and Sweden had put me to sleep. Now, we are almost at the end of the journey.

The young woman who so kindly made room on her bench seat is still sitting right next to me, still not looking at me. Her long black hair, deep tan, makeup, and nice clothing give me no clue if she even speaks English. I try to break the ice.

I say hello. I wait a moment and ask her what country she is from.

"I am Swedish," she says in perfect English.

"You don't look Swedish," is my impulsive, insensitive, ignorant reply. She is giving me a bad look. I have hurt her feelings.

I can be so stupid. Why would I think she couldn't be Swedish? Was it just because she's not blonde? What put that idea in my brain? Why did those words come out of my mouth? I am sorry for speaking without thinking and hurting her feelings but apologizing is not going to change what she thinks of me now. I apologize anyway.

I know too many people back home who always want to know, about anyone they meet, "Are they Americans?" or "What country are his/her parents from?" (And what religion are they?) They think they have learned something about the stranger's character based on the answers. (White people amaze my black roommate, Ed.)

I hope I do not have that bad habit. When I meet someone new, I don't want to have any prejudice. I have learned every nationality (and religion) is capable of anything, good and bad. And I know Swedes are not just blue-eyed blondes. However, my question and response revealed me as ignorant.

I embarrassed myself. And after hitchhiking around Europe for the last two months I know better.

1968 Europeans are amazing on a person-to-person level. Two generations ago, many leaders on this continent promoted ignorance and prejudice to advance their own power. (Not just Hitler.) They brought hate and war down on everyone.

Between the two world wars, international relations resembled relations between *pirates*. Poland invaded Russia and took land. Italy invaded Albania. Italy and Germany sent forces to help Franco win in Spain. Germany seized Austria without a fight. Hungary took land in Czechoslovakia. People thought using force to advance their national interests was normal and without serious consequence.

For security, countries relied on bigger weapons and secret alliances. Distrust among nationalities prevented cooperation on tariffs and trade, which would have improved everyone's life. There were frequent reports of discrimination against minority populations in many countries. Germany strongly protested the maltreatment of German speaking people in Poland and Czechoslovakia. People who disliked Germans thought they made it all up.

Then, in March of 1938, Germany took over part of Czechoslovakia with the *consent* of France and Great Britain.

No country intervened to stop any invasion or takeover. Austria, Britain, Czechoslovakia, France, Germany, Italy, Poland, and Romania were all democracies, at least at the beginning. Political parties and competitive elections chose national leaders.

Too many people voted according to their ignorance and prejudice. They believed lies about other people, and other countries. The most costly war in human history was the result.

The British and French declared war on Germans when Germans slaughtered the Poles. Hungarians fought Yugoslavs, who butchered Italians, who marched against Greeks. Germans invaded almost everybody except the Italians, Swiss and Swedes. Russians attacked the Finns, Latvians, Lithuanians, Poles, Estonians and Romanians. Romanians invaded Russia joined by the Germans, Hungarians and Italians.

Italy invaded Southern France on June 10, 1940 while Germany attacked in the north. On both fronts during the spring of 1940, Germans and Italians killed 92,000 French soldiers.

The world paid a high price for ignorance and prejudice. An accepted estimate {from the World Book Encyclopedia} of military and civilian deaths caused by the six years of World War 2 is an incomprehensible *55 million men, women, and children.*

It is now twenty-three years since the war ended. Most Europeans have learned not to prejudge someone according to their country of origin. Young people from every country are traveling everywhere through the generosity of other Europeans who have cars. Germans are hitchhiking in France, French are hitchhiking in Italy, Italians are hitchhiking in Spain...

I heard stories from many European hitchhikers. I know what happened to me happened to them too.

Drivers frequently went miles beyond their destinations to drop us off at well-traveled intersections instead of deserted back roads. People took us home. They fed us and let us stay overnight in their houses. However, no hitchhiker told a story about a driver as nice as Barbara, who drove me from Narbonne to her chateau near Nice.

I still feel bad about hurting the feelings of the

young Swedish woman and apologize again, but she keeps her eyes averted. I leave. I take my backpack and bedroll and go out on deck.

Just a few dozen miles from Copenhagen, the weather is completely different. It is sunny and warm. The air smells good, of the sea. The land of Sweden begins at the nearby beach. I see some low old buildings and a few modern ones. We are approaching the docks of Malmo.

We arrive in the late afternoon. Customs takes a few minutes. I exchange some dollars for Swedish kroners and get something to eat for lunch. After all this traveling my money is getting low. Warning! Do not run out of money before returning to Paris and catching the flight home.

I have the fantasy about not returning, hitchhiking for a year instead. The idea of going south to Greece and then going to the Middle East for the winter intrigues me. I have heard from other hitchhikers that the road to India is completely open now. Others have done it, hitchhiked through Turkey, Iraq, Iran, Afghanistan, Pakistan, and on to India and Tibet. And returned. All those countries are at peace now and their borders are open.

Hitchhiking to India or Egypt is a beautiful fantasy to have while sitting in the sun on a park bench in Sweden and eating a good lunch. Then, lunch is finished. I tell myself to go back and complete my senior year at college but I am not convinced.

Malmo is not a big tourist destination. There is not much to do after lunch. I remember my quest. I dig out the phone number, find a pay phone, build up my confidence, and make the call. An operator comes on and asks me, first in Swedish then in English for money. I put a few coins in the slot.

A man answers, maybe her dad and he speaks English too. He says Ice is home. After a few questions, he gives her the phone.

I think she sounds glad to hear from me. She says I should spend the night in Malmo and visit her tomorrow in Gothenburg. Her part-time summer job is over at 5 PM so I should meet her at her parents' house after five. Ice gives me her address again and for directions says, "Just ask anybody where the street is. They will show you." Why am I not surprised?

After we hang up I'm wet with sweat. I am thrilled with my success. However, where will I spend the night?

Back at the customs house, I ask the man behind the counter if Malmo has a youth hostel. The hostel system is great. Hostels are the backbone of traveling in Europe on $6 a day.

He tries to help. He speaks a few words in English, "Look for the student house" and points at the map on the wall. The place is on it. So is a bus route that goes from here to there. I take the next bus.

When we get to the student house, my hopes for a place to stay begin to fade. It looks nothing like a youth hostel. I see a modern apartment building at least 10 stories high. I walk up to it. I can't get in. The front has a buzzer entrance system. The building has no lobby, no signs for traveling students to read, no receptionist. I hope this doesn't mean I will have to sleep in a park again.

In Germany last week, I had to sleep outdoors in the city of Kassel. My driver left me at the train station there late at night. His advice was to get a bed at the hostel and in the morning, go see Kassel's international art show. But the hostel was closed for the night. And there were no hotels with vacancies because of all the people coming to see the art.

The man selling train tickets told me police arrest people who sleep in the station and pointed me in the direction of the park. When it started raining, I went under a bush and rolled up in my bedroll and poncho. Sleeping alone outdoors can be great. I did it many times. In the mornings, it was exhilarating to wake up. I felt like an explorer in the wilderness.

In Kassel, I woke up a wet and cold explorer. With a crowd, I explored this famous art event, the

Fourth Documenta. People walked around and saw modern art from all over the world in various public buildings. I looked at some big bright cartoon paintings with "Bang" and "Pow" written on them and some colorful electrical mechanisms.

Unfortunately, the bright paintings were hanging in poorly lit, narrow, elementary school hallways and the mechanisms sat quietly in the school basement without electricity to make them gyrate. I never got dry. The day in Kassel was a total down.

Tonight in Malmo, I don't want to sleep outdoors and be an explorer. I do not want to be wet and cold. I feel like having the companionship of other people to talk with, and listen to. I am in Europe for the experience and being alone is missing something. I need a shower and want to eat. If I have to pay for a hotel today, I will be poor tomorrow.

I am standing, looking at the building, wondering what to do next. The alternatives are bleak. My backpack and bedroll are at my feet.

The first person out the door is a very well dressed Swedish woman just a few years older than I am. She asks me something in Swedish. Then she demands, in English, "What are you doing in front of my building." Without attitude, I explain.

The student house turns out to be a college dormitory. The residents during the summer session are teachers who are earning credit towards advanced degrees. She says, "Come in. I will find you a place to stay for the night."

Before I know it, we are walking in the hallway together and she is telling me we are going back to her dorm room. The hallway is one long corridor. It is unlike any dormitory hallway I have ever seen. Not only is this one super-clean, it has no graffiti. And there are no notices, advertisements, or bulletin boards cluttering the walls.

No one else is around. We walk to the elevators. We go in and up and get off at her floor.

Her dorm room is a surprise. It is actually big. It is fully decorated, has artwork on the walls, and personal possessions arranged neatly on every horizontal surface. She has several chairs around the room, a large chest of drawers covered with cotton lace, and a small table. She has the curtains drawn making the room dark. It smells nice. I can see she likes candles. And her bed is made.

This woman is full of surprises. She turns around, faces me, and suggests I might like to take a shower. "Yes. I would like a shower."

She leads me down the hallway to where the showers are and shows me how to adjust the warm water. She is very close and smells very good. She is shorter than I am and her clothes are tight.

"I will have to bring you a clean towel," she says as she goes out the bathroom door.

My mind explodes with "What did she just say?" but I know-full-well exactly what she said. Immediately I am peeling my clothes off. I begin taking a wonderful shower.

CHAPTER 4

BARBARA, HER PROFESSOR, AND THE CHATEAU

I am taking the best shower I have ever had. And it is not because my last shower was in Berlin four days ago. Shampooing my hair again, scrubbing every inch of skin, I want to be ready for whatever happens when the towel arrives. I am entertaining a delicious fantasy.

I am also stretching my imagination. That Swedish woman was not coming on to me. She is attractive looking but that does not make me attractive to her. She started bossing me around from the moment we met. I do not want to think about that reality but I know what it means. She is acting like one of my older sisters.

This is not the first time a woman about the age of my older sisters helped me while I was hitchhiking around Europe. I start thinking about Barbara, my driver from Narbonne to Nice.

If you look on a map those two cities are hundreds of miles apart. Barbara and I traveled together across France's Mediterranean Coast, from near Spain to near Italy.

We met on my second day hitchhiking alone. This was after I woke up in the little café on the mountainside, next to the fork in the road. And after I had coffee and sweet rolls for breakfast.

Across the road from the café, a farmer picked me up and drove me down to the coast. I got out where the road across Southwestern France ends a few miles north of Narbonne. It was still early in the morning but the air was hot and humid already.

Immediately I started hitchhiking east on a dusty two lane blacktopped road. Cars sped by as I walked backwards with my arm stretched out and thumb up. Smoke was in the air. So far, no place in Europe had looked like this.

I was hitchhiking alongside two 19th Century villas with crumbling stucco walls. Something had smashed in the gates to one of them. Vines and weeds covered both places. At one time, they were the homes of wealthy people. Now they looked abandoned.

I thought I would have my first view of the blue Mediterranean at Narbonne but it was not where it should be according to my map. Instead, I saw the dry bed of a lake.

In the other direction, I saw the long mountain ridge I had just descended with the farmer. On the land between the parched earth and the mountains, many new factories had been built. Their tall chimneys poured white smoke over everything. Their presence dominated the view.

This area was mostly industrial and polluted. I was walking through hot air that smelled like something rotten burning. It was an oppressive, depressing morning air.

I was glad to see a car stop before too much time went by. And when I saw it was an attractive young French woman with long black hair who stopped her car for me I was thrilled.

She did not open the door right away. She pointed at me and asked out the window, "American?"

When I said "yes," she gave me a big smile.

She motioned "get in" with her hand. Her car was another small French Citroen with an open sunroof and more importantly, padded seats. I could sit back and enjoy the ride.

Communication however, was immediately a challenge. She told me her name was Barbara but she

spoke almost no English just some Spanish. My
Spanish and her Spanish were about equal. Since
neither of us spoke the other's native language, we
conversed in Spanish. We did double interpretations of
everything. And some misinterpretations. We were
soon laughing at ourselves. We were having fun.

Then she stopped laughing and pulled her
dress down to cover her knees. And with one hand on
the wheel, she used the other to button the top two
buttons of her blouse. However, she continued to
smile and talk. Barbara even tried to teach me French.
She pronounced the French words for things we saw
and I tried to.

As we drove along the industrial road, even
with all the windows down and sunroof open, the
oppressive air stayed on our faces. Then we sped up.
The road straightened and we entered ancient, rural
France. The wind blew in the side windows and
pushed our hair around. The hot, stinking air was left
behind.

I was never on this road before but I knew
what happened here. I remembered some of my
European history class. Three thousand years ago,
Greeks took this land from the local people and built
colonies. Then the Romans took it from the Greeks.
Then the Visigoths who conquered Rome left a path of
destruction down the coast. They even overwhelmed

the defenders of Narbonne and killed or enslaved every man, women, and child.

This coast road was how Moslem armies invaded France. The narrow strip of flat land between the mountains and the sea is a natural invasion route. And it works in either direction.

In 1938, the army loyal to the Spanish government did not invade France. They retreated into France after their defeat by Franco and the bombing by Hitler's Luftwaffe.

Thirty years have passed and many former Spanish soldiers still live in southeastern France. Even after three decades, there has been no amnesty. These men and their families are now waiting for Franco to die so they can go home.

I figured Barbara gave rides to hitchhikers frequently. She liked to talk. She never touched me, not even on the shoulder but she was very friendly. I thought here I am, just a visitor to her country and she is being so nice to me.

We stopped for sodas and gas. I had more Spanish pesos in my pocket than French francs. Barbara refused to take any contribution. She paid.

After asking if I wanted to see the ocean, Barbara detoured off the main road to show me the Mediterranean. We drove along sand dunes, beaches, and the surf for almost an hour. We passed several campgrounds and hundreds of vacationers but no big hotels or any beachside honky-tonk. The French had occupied this coastline for thousands of years and there were still many miles of natural, unspoiled, beautiful beaches.

Frequently we drove by places to pull over and park. I told Barbara I wanted to go into the ocean. She asked what I would wear and nixed the idea of me jumping in wearing the cut-off jeans I had on. "nada" didn't work either. I realized I never saw a clothing optional-nudist beach. Everyone was wearing bathing suits. There were lots of families.

Did I regret not bringing a bathing suit? Disappointment did not cross my mind. I had only started hitchhiking yesterday and already I was having the ideal day. This beautiful woman was driving and her car was cool. The rays through the sunroof had me smiling. We were heading in the right direction, towards Rome. I was seeing interesting things I had never seen before. I was in hitchhiker heaven.

We went over many bridges. We drove through many small, old towns, and several big cities. We saw a castle on a hilltop and an old fort in a harbor. We passed donkeys pulling carts and children riding bicycles. A Ferrari and several Porsches passed us.

We stopped for lunch at an old restaurant that Barbara had been to before. Here I learned a little about my benefactor. She was married and her husband was an artist. She used to be a student at a University. She and her husband had been in Paris during the spring riots. She had traveled to Spain "por trabajo," for work. I did not understand what kind of work but I did understand she wasn't looking for a job. She had a job but I could not translate what it was she did.

I did not press Barbara for explanations. We had a language problem so I only asked easy questions. I wanted to be fun to be with. Barbara left the table to go make a phone call. I paid the bill with all my Spanish pesos. I got a terrible exchange rate but so what, I will never go back to Spain until the dictator is dead.

Barbara returned. We went outside to her car and the beautiful day. She told me we were going to make a detour to visit a college professor in Marseilles. She did not say why and I did not ask. Barbara said I could stay in the car, but she also said he knew I was with her and he welcomed my visit.

You bet I wanted to see the professor. His field was Economics. My college degree will be in Economics; my major is Political Science my desired minor, History. I love this stuff.

I even carried a radical economics pamphlet with me. I was reading it for a third time. It is about who will dominate the world twenty years from now. It was a difficult read but the author made predictions, like Nostradamus.

Some women told me the author had mega charisma like Charlton Heston, the actor. More than a few people said he looked just like Vladimir Ilych Lenin, the leader of the Russian communist revolution. He gave great speeches. He was the kind of a guy people loved or hated. He went by several names. I knew people who called him Lyn Marcus but he had a different name on this pamphlet.

Marseilles is about as old as European cities can be. The Greeks founded it 600 years before the Christian era began. The city was always an important seaport and now is a big industrial zone. As we approached, I could see giant oil refineries smoking up the coastline. It was rush hour. We skipped the center of town and drove around north to the hilly, expensive, residential area. The sun was still shining and sky still blue.

To say the professor lived the good life is an understatement. Barbara parked her Citroen on a street lined with large villas. We were on a hillside overlooking the city of Marseilles. I had no idea she was taking me to a pool party at his house.

We walked around to the back. Dozens of people had come to this party. A few were swimming;

most were sitting around the pool. Some were surrounding one man. They were young; he was over 50. His hair was white and he was sitting in a lawn chair with a drink in his hand. I saw him and thought, "This must be the professor."

Barbara went right over to him. He stood up. He welcomed her with kisses on both cheeks. They talked (in French), and she introduced me. I was received with a warm handshake and big smile. He spoke English fluently and asked me to sit down. A young man brought me a beer. Barbara left us.

The professor wanted to know where I was from and what I was studying. Those answers were easy. I wanted to know the real story behind all the recent rioting and street warfare in Paris. Those answers took longer.

The professor began by telling me on May third the students started it, "one-two-three."

One. Eight student leaders arrived at the Sorbonne (university) in Paris to spread the word about their disciplinary hearings. They faced expulsion because they led protests against the French educational system and the Vietnam War. They knew school authorities wanted to make examples of them.

Two. Dozens of students found themselves being taken away and forced into police vans during the rally supporting the eight student leaders. News about police arresting students on campus and rumors it was for no reason, spread quickly. People blocked the vans from leaving with the arrested students. Tear gas was shot into the crowd. Tear gas did not work.

Three. Thousands of students spontaneously started gathering in the small courtyard where all this was happening. They demanded police release the students in the vans. There was a standoff for a long time. Then riot policeman swinging nightsticks attacked the front ranks of students. However, people could not run away because thousands in back were pressing forward to see what was happening.

The police who charged into the crowd soon found themselves surrounded by people who were resisting, defending themselves out of necessity. The police had expected students to run. Students fought them to a draw. The police withdrew. They shot off water cannons and nausea gas and attacked again, harder.

As the crowd was broken up into smaller groups, fighting moved to the wide boulevards and narrow alleys of the Latin Quarter in Paris. Groups of students bombarded police lines with projectiles from the street: paving stones, splintered posts, bricks, metal, etc. Molotov cocktails, made from gasoline siphoned out of gas tanks into bottles and cans exploded near police positions. Between morning and nightfall, a peaceful neighborhood had changed into a dangerous battle zone.

Hours passed before police restored order on the streets. It was good no one died but hospitals in Paris treated scores of students, police, and innocent residents. Police arrested five hundred students.

The professor told me the attack on the demonstrators gained students the sympathy of the middle class. And the fact that the students fought back gained them the respect of the working class.

The students lit a match. The unemployed, the low paid workers, and high school students from poor neighborhoods became dynamite as they joined university students at daily protests in the streets.

"The next things that happened went beyond easy description," the professor said. Later, I put together more causes and effects of the May explosion.

Young people hated the rigid French educational system. Advancement was determined by standardized testing. If you came from a poor school chances were you would do poorly. Many schools were overcrowded. If you flunked a "sudden death" exam you could be thrown out of school. Most jobs available paid you very low wages and any hope of promotion was a fantasy. Students were angry.

During the 1960's French workers' pay

remained stagnant while economic wealth increased 50%. The well off were better off than ever while millions of French citizens earned the minimum wage of 42 cents an hour. Many millions of full time workers took home a subsistence paycheck. Unions went on strike to gain wage increases but the government used the law (and police) to break the strikes.

The conservative government of President Charles de Gaulle constantly demanded austerity at workers' expense. They even increased deductions from paychecks for health care. Workers were angry.

No wonder students and workers exploded. On May 6, Paris experienced an even bigger more violent street battle. Police and thousands of demonstrators fought one another from before noon to the middle of the night.

Then demonstrations by students and workers started happening in other French cities besides Paris. One of the slogans of the demonstrators was, "THE FATE OF THE PEOPLE DOES NOT INTEREST OUR LEADERS."

On May 10, the national French student organization called for a demonstration in Paris' Latin Quarter, on the Left Bank. They had three demands: the government should re-open the universities, withdraw security police from the Latin Quarter, and release all demonstrators previously arrested.

The Paris Chief of Police labeled demonstrators "subversives." Maybe he thought his forces were ready for anything this time.

The leaders of the demonstration said they would only leave the streets if the police withdrew first. Maybe they thought they were ready for anything too.

At the beginning, the protestors just demonstrated. There were speeches. People waved signs. The crowd grew beyond anyone's expectation. The police just watched. The standoff showed no signs of resolving itself.

At two in the morning special security police charged into the mass of people to disperse them. Fists, sticks, rocks, and paving stones repelled their attack. The demonstrators appeared organized this time. They pushed cars into the streets, overturned them, and used them as shields and barricades. As demonstrators retreated, they set many cars on fire. The fighting and control of the streets went back and forth from barricade to barricade, almost until dawn.

No one proved ready for what thirty thousand angry people could do. The May 12, 1968 New York Times reported 788 cars and trucks burned or damaged, 468 arrests, and 367 injuries with serious injury to 13 policemen.

The arrested included former supporters of de Gaulle, people who were non-political the week before, and people who previously thought demonstrations and protests were a waste of time.

The professor said, "Things went beyond easy description." I say the different ways the French people and their conservative government reacted to these events went beyond anyone's prediction.

Shortly after the May 10 demonstration, French union leaders called for a 24-hour general strike and big labor demonstrations across the country on May 13. That day, there was a demonstration in Paris with almost one million people marching, demanding change. Many other French cities also had huge demonstrations.

On May 14, many workers did not go back to work. They took the general strike beyond the one-day event called by union leaders. Three million workers stayed away from their jobs, then five million. One-week later eight million workers were on strike in sympathy with low paid workers, in support of students' rights, and with their own grievances.

Many strikers supported President de Gaulle up to then because the old World War 2 hero made them feel better. Now they were in the streets and on strike for a cause. Victory would make their lives better.

Union leaders saw the light and got behind the nation-wide general strike. Food delivery became organized. Truckers stopped non-food deliveries. Retail clerks went out and department stores closed. Poor farmers blocked highways with tractors. Assembly lines came to a halt. Some workers occupied their factories to prevent scab labor from reopening them and to protect their leaders from being arrested at home. Even bank workers stayed home, shutting down the banks. Then television workers joined the strike and TV's went blank across the country.

Many people only stayed home because workers for the trains, subways, and buses were on strike and there was no way to get to their jobs. Many consumers did not care about low wages for people who waited on them in restaurants and stores or made their appliances and cars. They hated the inconvenience the strike caused.

French government ministers called the demonstrators "mere troublemakers" and demanded adherence to "law and order." They were not negotiating.

Charles de Gaulle had been the leader of the French Resistance during the war and always a popular leader with his countrymen. He asked the French to allow democracy to work. He called for a referendum putting everything up for a vote. (Exactly what would be voted on, "Go back to work for subsistence wages?")

The leader of the unions said workers would not return to work for "Vague promises of future reforms." He told newspapers the strike might last several weeks. Those uncaring consumers started to take notice and take sides.

An alliance of French corporate leaders called for "No new intolerable charges upon industry." They knew the general strike was a threat to people whose high incomes came from big profits paid out by French corporations.

Something had to change; conservative groups started organizing counter-demonstrations against the strike.

What came next looked like a civil war. Security forces, hired thugs, and provocateurs all over France tried to break up student-worker meetings and marches. Enough men and women on strike actually had to physically fight back or everyone had to go home and give up on this chance for a better life.

It became clear French workers and students would fight back. They kept up the pressure on the government. New demonstrations occurred. Picket lines strengthened. Occupations of factories, colleges, and high schools increased. The general strike expanded. By the third week of May 1968 the number of injured was in the thousands; killed were men on both sides, and twelve million workers were on strike.

That was estimated to be two-thirds the entire workforce. The economy of France was no longer producing wealth for anyone.

De Gaulle never called in the army. Maybe he worried the soldiers would slaughter demonstrators, or join them. Either would be much more trouble. It was not worth the risk.

On May 23, the French police organization gave the government notice they would not be willing to fight against demonstrators indefinitely. Their declaration even expressed sympathy for the strikers' demands. (However, this came from local police not the hated special security police who lived in barracks and were similar to military units.)

At the party, students from Marseilles began to surround the professor and me. As we talked, one young man with long black hair and wearing a black shirt and black pants began translating into French what the professor and I said so other students could understand.

I told them street fighting in Paris made front-page headlines in the United States. On the TV news with Walter Cronkite, the violent battles between students and police were one of the two top stories in May. Video images of crowds hurling rocks and firebombs at police in Paris were every bit as compelling as video images of soldiers fighting house to house against the Vietcong army living inside Saigon. However, demonstrations in other French cities and the nationwide general strike were not big stories on the news.

The student in black told me the docks and refineries in Marseilles shut down completely. He and other young people at the party were proud of how the citizens of their city stood up against the national government, demanding it serve the people.

I told them I never learned how or why the events of May ended. I had to study for my year-end exams. And when the air force began bombing poor neighborhoods in Saigon, I started passing out anti-draft literature where draftees were being inducted into the army. "Will someone tell me what happened in France?"

The professor said President de Gaulle gave in on May 25. He enacted a 35% increase of the minimum industrial wage and wage increases of 7% to 10% for all workers. He promised more spending on education, and granted pardons for thousands of students arrested and still in jail.

Many workers returned to their jobs. Many others defied their own union leaders and continued occupying the factories. Universities remained shut down. Cities across France still experienced massive pro-strike and anti-strike rallies.

However, students and workers had lost some advantage. In late May and early June street fighting became even more violent and the police more repressive. "Extremist" leaders were "removed" from union meetings and from college campuses. Special security police viciously attacked the remaining strikers, retaking one occupied factory at a time. These workers fought back bitterly. For the first time, people used guns and set off dynamite.

On June 23, 1968, Twenty-two million French people elected representatives for their National Assembly (congress). The winners were Charles de Gaulle and his Gaullist party. That was the end.

Like my professors back home, the French professor looked at the past and tried to write history by applying his opinion to events. He told me students and workers could have toppled the government of France if the strike continued. He said the students had the sympathy of the people and the forces of truth and justice on their side. The French unions had legitimate leaders with a broad base of support. Workers did not have to settle for such a small piece of the pie (18 more cents/hour.)

The young man from Marseilles predicted businesses would raise prices more than 10% in the next two years. If union leaders had really been interested in helping workers, they should have maintained the strike and now would be forming the new government of France. They lost the chance to change how the French economic system distributed the wealth of the nation.

The professor spoke to us about how the unions became a powerful political force equal to bankers and corporate chiefs because of the May riots. He hoped everyone learned wages must rise with prices and profits or France will face problems like this again.

The professor predicted no strikes or riots would disrupt my travels in France during the summer. [He was right.] He was sure the universities would reopen in September and the system would change very slowly [right again.] He saw the liberalization of the communist regime in Czechoslovakia continuing. [He was tragically wrong.] He said a "third way," that blended the freedom of capitalism and the economic security of socialism would become a real movement for change in the world over the next few years.

The students from Marseilles were interested in university students in the U.S. and the rioting against the "American War" (in Vietnam.) I told them only a small fraction of students actively opposed the war. [I was right.] I said Americans of all ages and incomes were demonstrating [Right again.] Riots, like the street fighting in Paris or the bombing of government buildings would never happen in America. [I was wrong on both.] I predicted when my generation took over we would pass legislation to change taxation to make greed serve the common good.

We talked for a long time, more time than I ever talked with any professor back at my university. I told him about predictions in the economics pamphlet I carried with me. It predicted multi-national corporations cared more about profit than our country and would soon be exporting millions of jobs of American workers overseas [right.] It foresaw a time when Americans would be working more hours then their parents worked to achieve a middle-class standard of living. [That happened.] The author predicted greater wealth for the wealthy and an economic depression, worse than the one that started in 1929, starting any day now. The author used the name "Lyndon LaRouche" on this pamphlet.

The professor seemed very interested in the pamphlet. He asked. "Could Mr. LaRouche win an election?"

"I don't know-maybe if he is right about another big depression."

Barbara came back and told me she did not want to drive in the dark. We both got something to eat and then said our goodbyes to the professor. He said he was interested in the economics pamphlet so I got it out of my backpack.

I told him "Maybe putting this pamphlet into your hands is my destiny; it is why Barbara stopped for me this morning outside Narbonne." This was just a joke. I said it with a laugh.

The professor laughed with me but then said our meeting was not a coincidence. He explained how Barbara's father had fought with U.S. troops in the Second World War and had told her to be nice to Americans. She was thinking about him on the road out of Narbonne when she saw a young man hitchhiking who looked like an American. Her father was why she stopped for me. The professor said Barbara told him she had never picked up a hitchhiker before.

The two of them talked some more, even loudly, and turned and looked at me several times. I became uncomfortable. "What is this about?" I was thinking.

The professor told me I was very lucky. Barbara was inviting me to spend the night at her chateau; it was over 500 years old and in a beautiful village one hour north of Nice. I would meet her husband. In the morning, she would have to go to work but she would show me the road to take to get to where I was going first. I would have no trouble completing my journey. He said Barbara was doing this at some risk but it was important to her.

I asked no questions. I accepted Barbara's invitation with many thanks.

The professor did not need to tell me this was special any more than he had to tell me to be good. As I left, he told me both. He was Barbara's friend.

Barbara and I left the party and Marseilles. We said little to one another. I think we were both tired. What the professor said about Barbara's motivations produced strong emotions in me. I thought about my two uncles who were in the army during WWII. I grew up hearing about the sacrifices millions of people made to win the war against fascism. Every night there were shows on TV about the war. They were never sarcastic or funny {in the 1950's and 60's.} I watched plenty.

I could only imagine what Barbara learned from her father about WW2. As we drove along, I did not have a clue about what she was thinking but I was very comfortable with the direction we were going.

It did get dark. Barbara put the headlights on. Then she turned them off to save the battery. With the headlights on, we could see up the road about fifty feet ahead of us. Everything else was very dark. With the headlights off, the moon and the stars provided our light. We could see far up the road, deep into the woods, and across the farmland. Whenever we saw the headlights of another car approaching, Barbara always turned on her headlights. Then she turned them off after the car had passed. Instantly, a car with no headlights shot by us on the other side of the narrow road. I did not even see it coming. If we had collided, I would not have known what hit me. Barbara was affected by the close call too and kept the lights on after that.

We got closer to her chateau. Our car climbed a hill and she parked. We walked up the hill a considerable distance farther to an old, tall, stone building. Barbara took me to the back door. We entered the kitchen and immediately climbed a narrow curved staircase to a room on the third floor.

It was dark. Barbara lit a candle and said I was to stay there. She told me she wanted to go get her husband because he spoke English and we could all talk together.

A long time went by, then SHOCK! This man jumped into the doorway with a SHOUT! Barbara was behind him. He assumed the posture of a weigh lifter and had a large stone block in his hands. He started pumping it up and down, very aggressively.

I moved back. Barbara said he was her husband. He did not need English to communicate. He stood in the doorway and looked angry. He breathlessly said the block was from the cobblestone streets of Paris. He had pulled it up during a riot and brought it home.

"Why?" was the first thing I asked him.

"Because I wanted to," was his reply. The candlelight made this minute even more spooky.

We did not engage in conversation. He told me I should not walk around the house at night. I should not even go out of the room. Large dogs lived in the house and no one could predict how they would react to a stranger.

"What do you need?" he asked.

I said, "I need to go to the bathroom."

He took me around the corner. The hallway had electric lights. We went down to the second floor. This area looked recently renovated. The wide plank floors were beautifully stained and the old plaster walls were clean and smooth. The hallway sparkled with chandeliers, antiques and old paintings. It had a Persian carpet on the floor. The place was not a hotel; there were no room numbers on the doors; the bathroom was off the regular hallway. He waited while I used the bathroom. I was thinking, "His family or hers must have a lot of money."

On the way back to the bedroom, we said nothing. I was really wondering about him. When we got there, they both reminded me not to leave the

room. I should stay there and go to sleep. Barbara
wished me a good night and said she would get me in
the morning.

I had seen many movies about Transylvania
where a young traveler was in a similar situation. As a
child, I had frequent night terrors about monsters
under my bed. I slept curled up in the middle; if I got
too close to an edge I thought an awful creature would
drag me below to a horrible death. Every morning I
woke up and realized I had survived. By 1968 I had
stopped being afraid of the dark. I could sleep
anywhere.

At Barbara's chateau, in an old room with a
history of one hundred thousand nights, next to a
window that looked out onto acres of moonlit forest,
under a comforter that had a beautiful fragrance, I
blew out the candle and slept through the night.

When I woke up, I did have a problem. Dogs or
no dogs I had to go to the bathroom. As quietly as
possible, I re-traced my steps. No one saw me. I saw
no dogs. However when I returned, coffee and sweet
rolls were on the dresser.

Barbara came up later. We left the house via
the kitchen and a heavyweight woman wearing a white
hat and apron laughed at me (or us) as we went
outside.

Barbara and I walked on a cobblestone road

towards the way out of town. Many of the buildings were very old; maybe they were built before Christopher Columbus was born. Construction materials were chiseled stone blocks, rough bricks, and mortar. Some walls looked like old castle walls. Shops of artisans and craftspeople lined the street.

It was so early no one else was around. The shops were still closed. Barbara asked if I wanted to buy anything. Right there was a shoemaker's shop. I traveled with only one pair of shoes; the hiking boots I was wearing. My feet had already been hot for days and days; I needed to cool them off. I told her I needed sandals.

Hand made shoes and sandals were in the shop's small window. We found the door locked but we could hear a man hammering tacks and a radio playing.

Barbara knocked and he opened the door. The cobbler was an old man with white hair and skin like tan leather. He let us in and talked to Barbara. He spoke English to me. His shop smelled great. He looked as though he had made shoes all his life.

Barbara knew him. Of course she knew him; this ancient town was her town. She probably knew everybody.

The price of a beautiful pair of thick leather hand-made sandals was one hundred francs. That was about $20. He was willing to take American Express Traveler's Checks.

I explained I was a student; I was hitchhiking around Europe and had just enough money for $6 a day.

She told me she understood the problem of not having enough money. So did the shoemaker. He went into the back and brought out a pair of mass produced sandals. He encouraged me to try them on. They fit me fine. They were just a dollar and looked very cheap next to his hand-made sandals.

I actually had hundreds of dollars on me. The money was burning a hole in my pocket but I knew most of my journey was ahead of me; without dollars, I would go hungry.

I had a decision-making problem. $20 for sandals hand made by an old cobbler in an ancient French town, or $1 for perfectly comfortable sandals made in North Africa.

The old cobbler said the cheap ones were of good quality and would last all summer, no problem. Barbara told me $20 was his best price. He was not going to lower his price. It was $20 because of her. He might easily sell them for twice as much later that day. I paid my five francs.

Right there I tied my shoes to a ring on my backpack and let them dangle. I put on the sandals.

They felt good on my feet. Barbara, the shoemaker, and I were all smiling. He wished me a good adventure.

I was thinking, "Hitchhiking can't get any better than this."

Outside the store, Barbara and I said our goodbyes. We did not hug but she kissed me on both cheeks. I thanked her several times in English, Spanish, and French. I told her I could not thank her enough.

I also realized Barbara helped me because it was very important to her. I wanted to ask her about her father; was he was still alive? I was sorry I did not speak French. If I did, I would also ask if her husband was a crazy man.

We walked apart there, but the way out was not obvious. I turned around and yelled, "Barbara."

No one else was around. She looked at me, and I gave her a big shrug with my arms and shoulders. She knew what I wanted. She pointed at a gate through the old stone wall. From where I stood, only the bright, blue sky was visible through the opening. We waved goodbye.

The old road narrowed as it went under that stone arch. I walked out the gate. A steep incline propelled my feet quickly to the bottom of a hill and the highway to Nice.

Almost immediately, a car stopped. I was on the road to Nice and my next adventure. I never looked back.

Now I'm asking myself, "Would I have seen a medieval town with castle walls around it? Would it have looked like a picture in a storybook about kings, and knights, and crusaders, the stuff of legends?"

In this shower is the first time I have been thinking about Barbara's town since walking away from it. I would like an answer to my question. I must go back there and see it someday.

Right now, I am enjoying the warm water massaging my back. And I want to return to my fantasy.

CHAPTER 5

SWEDISH PARTY

I am taking this shower hoping I'm wrong about reality.

Whatever her motivation, this new Swedish woman has completely lifted my spirits. I thought acts of kindness towards complete strangers were rare in this world but I have been on the receiving end of one act of kindness after another all summer. Like Barbara's.

Thinking about Barbara is the first sentimental thinking I have done during the whole trip. Right now, I don't have much more than $20 to my name. If I had bought those sandals, I would be broke. I would have had to pass up going to Berlin. I was so glad that she and the shoemaker understood my financial restraint.

They showed respect for me even after they learned I did not have much money to spend.

Then it hits me; Barbara was an employee at the big chateau. Rich people drive cars that can rely on their headlights at night. Wealthy families want to impress visitors with their possessions; at a minimum, we would have walked through the main room on the way out.

Now I understand what the professor said about risk, and Barbara and I using the kitchen door, and the cook laughing at us, and even the dog thing. And her husband–body builder, he was totally upset. He couldn't even talk to me. He was afraid, jealous, insecure, and about me! Not the strongman type. Maybe he was angry with Barbara. The guy was an obsessive possessive uptight weakling. Artist my foot.

I am laughing out loud.

Someone has entered the shower room. I stop laughing. Over the curtain rod comes a fluffy, white towel and well, it's a man's voice asking if I am finished showering. Goodbye to that fantasy.

He asks me, "Why are you laughing?"

"I'm remembering someone I met in France," I answer. "It's funny."

He says a few students here are giving a party in honor of their foreign visitor. They are getting some food and drinks together. I should finish and come back to the room. They would like to hear about my funny, French friend.

I am wondering who this foreign visitor is. I get out of the shower, dry myself, and put on clean clothes left from the Berlin Laundromat. They feel good.

Six Swedish teachers and I are at this party, some men and some women. Everyone is just a few years older than I am but everyone looks very "adult." My brand new Swedish friend introduces me as her friend from the United States. Candles are burning. A hot plate has meatballs on it and there are other things to eat.

I notice some people are drinking Vodka straight. They have beer too, which I drink.

We all get some of the food. Everything tastes good. People tell me they are from all over Sweden. They did not know one another before they came to the summer program in Malmo. In just a week, they will all be back teaching at their schools.

I sit on a thick rug on the floor. Someone wants to know what I was laughing about in the shower. I tell them about Barbara's chateau and her husband. No one laughs.

I share something about our long ride together across southern France. They are not amused. I don't know if it was good they heard me laughing.

One man says if his wife brought home a

hitchhiker, he would not be so kind. Another man says the hitchhiker would be shown the exit.

One of the women says. "But you don't even have a wife. She may have her own ideas." Then she insults him about his ability to ever get a wife. People argue about equality in marriage. I do not have anything to say. This might be a long evening.

Someone asks what happened after I left the medieval town on the hill. The strangest thing happened. I arrived at the hostel in Nice and there was Jim, my college roommate. Of the dozens of big cities and hostels between Biarritz and Rome, we were in the same one at the same time.

Jim and I were glad to see each other. He crossed France even faster than I did and arrived in Nice the day before. His first ride was with a family in a large luxury car who drove him hundreds of miles. The next day he got one ride that took him directly to Nice. He was lucky. I was lucky. But I would not trade the whack-a-mole Frenchman or Barbara for a fast ride anywhere.

No one at the party had been to Nice. It is a resort for French and English families situated on the Mediterranean next to Monte Carlo and Italy.

Jim knew Nice. Since he had been to the center of town already, he showed me where to eat lunch. Then we walked to the Mediterranean. Smooth stones the size of sandwiches made up the beach. There was not a grain of sand out there. People were spreading their towels and lying down on the stones. Jim and I went back to where we were staying and talked.

Nice was my introduction to European hostels. I stayed at many of them this summer and every single one was different. I slept in a bed in an old mansion and on the floor of a gymnasium. One hostel I saw looked like an old hotel and I was inside an old farmhouse/new hostel in Florence. Some were so overcrowded people slept on the ground outside. In a few the showers were unusable or locked up.

Crowds of college age travelers were the only constant I saw in every hostel where I stayed and talking politics was what young people did.

I frequently heard American students asked, "Are you against the American war in Vietnam?" and "Have you ever been in a demonstration?" Vietnam and the French riots were hot topics. Some European students argued as if they were from "royal" families whose fortunes had waned but whose titles remained. Others sounded like they came from working class families loyal to the communist party of France or Italy. Interesting mix.

I am a card-carrying member of Students for a Democratic Society. (S.D.S.) There are almost one hundred thousand of us. We want more "Power to the

People." Students should be demanding more say about what happens in their schools and workers about their working conditions. Stop the war in Vietnam. Fight Racism. Agreement among S.D.S. members ends there. My organization stands up for everything good and fights against anything bad. {Yea, right.}

So at these hostels we had great "bull sessions." "What do you mean!?" was both a challenge and an invitation. Opinions were shared freely. Passions clashed with assumptions. Personal experience trumped conjecture. Speculation was obvious.

The hostel at Nice provided a great place for talking about the future. We sat in comfortable chairs on a large sun-lit patio. We were European and American students coming from many points of view.

"What would our generation do when we took power?" we wondered. Would we make our futures more secure with national health care and better social security? Europeans enjoyed this benefit already.

Some said democratic socialism always followed democracy. Others argued taxes took away from wealthy people what was theirs by right.

"Do we still need unions?" was another question we debated. Corporations will always share the profits from improved productivity, some people said. They argued workers shouldn't go out on strike. They can use the ballot box if pay raises don't keep up with inflation and profits go up every year.

Should government be the employer of last resort? Is it natural for wages to fall as low as people are willing to work for? What right does government have to set a minimum wage, guarantee everyone a job, or dictate a nation-wide pay raise?

Before the riots, conservatives ran France for a decade. Their economic policy was to keep wages low and profits high. The French never thought of having middle class taxpayers subsidize poverty paychecks of hard-working people with government handouts like food stamps, heating assistance, Section 8 housing vouchers, and medical care instead of having businesses pay wages their own workers could live on.

No one argued some businesses should profit from paying their own workers lower real wages than the previous generation was paid.

No one guessed we would live to see big bosses in the U.S. increase their own pay from 20 times more than the average employee earned to 100 times more.

One American at the hostel in Nice objected to politics. He wanted everything he could get his hands on and "To hell with the next guy," he said. "I only take care of myself." He chased a beautiful dream of vast wealth and power. I wondered if he was serious. {I wonder now if he is happy. He might be one of those executives serving time in a Federal penitentiary for stock fraud or for looting a giant corporation.}

The hostel at Nice was so crowded with new arrivals I had to roll out my bedroll on the porch and sleep outside. Every morning I had to walk over to the campground next door and share the bathroom facilities there.

Morning among the European campers was eye opening. Most were families living in tents. Their campsites were right next to each other. Moms wearing bathing suits cooked breakfasts on portable gas stoves; children ran around all over the place. The cinderblock bathhouse was crowded with men from different countries showering and shaving. Everyone seemed to get along fine.

I left Nice after a couple of days. Jim stayed but I wanted to get to Rome. On the eastern edge of Nice, I met a dozen hitchhikers who were trying to get rides. It was the road to Italy and I walked down that road backwards with my thumb out. I was trying to distance myself from the pack.

Eventually I was picked up. First, I thought I was lucky. Then after five minutes in the car, the driver dropped me off in the next town. I did not get another ride for a long time.

I must have walked twenty miles along the French coast. The road had rugged cliffs on one side and a sheer drop into the ocean on the other. For a while I walked backwards with my thumb out. Then I just walked. I carried my pack on my back with my bedroll and shoes tied below.

Many other people were also hiking along the coast road. There were places to sit down, and places to eat lunch and dinner.

I tell the Swedes, "France has a beautiful coastline. You should see it."

Day became night. France ended and I walked into the Independent Principality of Monaco.

I was getting really weary from a full day of walking so I sat down on a bench across the street from the Grand Casino of Monte Carlo. One minute later a police car pulled up and out came two men in black uniforms. They were policemen who went beyond asking questions.

They made me unroll my sleeping bag on the ground and then they emptied everything in my backpack on top of my bag. Do you have any idea how carefully organized everything was packed and squeezed into that thing? Were they just doing their jobs or was this harassment? They searched through my stuff. They ordered me to leave immediately or I would be arrested and put in jail.

I would have been very happy to move on immediately, but first I had to re-pack everything. And they stood there, towering over me. Not everything fit!

Do they have bail in Monaco? I never found out. I sweated for the next five minutes and left.

The Swedes are not surprised. One teacher tells me, "You shouldn't hitchhike at night in Sweden either. It's against the law in some cities and if you are arrested you will go straight to jail for two weeks."

Another says that the nickname of the Swedish police is "Our Gestapo." Some people laugh.

"They like to enforce the law," someone adds.

"Sweden is nervous about hitchhikers," my friend says. "They are associated with crime, like gypsies." But she never really heard of, or read in the newspaper about crimes committed by hitchhikers.

Someone else says, "I heard about hitchhikers being driven far off the main road and just left in the Swedish forest. They have to walk all day just to get back to where they started."

That scares me.

We talk about college. A college education in Sweden is expensive. I am surprised, "I thought college was free in Sweden, like in California."

I hear Swedish universities are reserved for Swedes who can pay. Someone whispers, "Or whose family can afford it."

A man asks me, "Did you get a ride to the border between Italy and France; did anyone pick you up in the dark?"

I actually got two rides after walking away from in front of the casino. The first was from an old Frenchman who drove me from Monaco all the way to the crossing point. After I got out, he made a u-turn and drove back into France. He went out of his way for me! Then I walked passed French customs without anyone stopping me and went into the Italian customs house. The official looked at my passport, didn't stamp it, and sent me out the door.

There was no town at the border just a road. There was no place to convert a traveler's check into Italian lira. At least the area was very well lit up; drivers could see me. I started hitchhiking again.

An Italian man picked me up. He was tired. I was tired. We agreed to stop at the next motel. He and I split the cost of a room. The charge was only one dollar each. The cheapest room on the other side of the border would have cost us at least ten dollars. We slept.

All at once the Swedes are throwing questions at me. "Weren't you afraid of him?" type of questions. Someone asks, "What if he killed you?" Too many questions are coming at me. Everyone thinks it is a bad idea to hitchhike at night.

Changing the subject would be a good idea. I ask if they would like to hear about when I shared a hotel room an American con artist. Talking about that guy might take the heat off me.

One of the Swedes says, "Tell us about him."

In Germany, when I went to Munich I had no choice about sharing a room. The hostels were filled. Most hotels had "no vacancy" signs out in front. When I finally did find a vacancy, the clerk told me the next customer would get the other bed in my room. I asked; he said he was talking about the next male customer.

Soon a man my age came in with two black suitcases. He was wearing a suit and tie and talking excitedly. One of the things he said was he had just arrived on the train from Moscow. His appearance and the way he talked were very different from any other young traveler I had met so far.

Moscow was a disaster area according to him. He walked a few miles away from the Red Square tourist area and saw the ugly underbelly of the communist super-power. Poor people and dilapidated housing were everywhere. At the local train station, people were living on the platforms. Entire families were there cooking, sleeping, and waiting for the government to do something.

I stop the story and tell the Swedes this is also happening in Washington D.C tonight. Except in D.C.

thousands of poor are living in tents right next to the beautiful memorial for Abraham Lincoln, not in a train station. They say nothing.

When I told my Munich roommate about the Poor People's Campaign and Resurrection City USA in Washington D.C. he just kept talking.

He said, "Tourist Moscow is beautiful. The central train station in Moscow looks like a palace but at this local train station, people are desperate for food. They are selling their personal possessions to buy things to eat. They are selling jewelry, artwork, and WWII stuff for almost nothing."

He had stuff with him. He opened one bag and showed me watches and jewelry. I couldn't tell if they were valuables or cheap fakes.

He said when you exit the U.S.S.R. by train the Soviet border police do not search you. He had just arrived from Moscow and now he was going back to buy as many World War 2, German Lugar automatic pistols as he could bring back in two suitcases. He said he would make a fortune selling them in the States.

He wanted me to go back with him. If I took a thousand dollars, I would make fifty thousand dollars. He was ready to go. He was mailing the stuff he bought back home tomorrow and leaving for Russia after that.

He asked, "Don't you want to go?"

This was how he talked after knowing me for less than five minutes.

He said, "Russians are stupid. They have no idea how valuable those Lugars are" and "I can make you rich."

I told him I did not have the money.

"$300 would be enough," he said. "Call your parents."

"I'm not calling my parents for money!"

I did not even ask my parents to help pay for this trip. My job last summer in a factory and my two student jobs (serving food in the college cafeteria and putting books back on library shelves) got me the money. Only my Uncle Joe, the army veteran gave me any money.

Before our plane left for Europe, at a family party my Uncle Joe gave Jim and me $20 each {Because of inflation, $20 in 1968 equals over $100 in year 2005 dollars.} He told us to do something special with it.

At that party, my elderly grandmother told me how proud she was of me. She had come to the United States from Europe in 1911 and I was the first member of our family to ever go back as a tourist. She gave me these words of warning, "Be careful. Don't believe everything people say to you."

Her warning sure applied to this guy. Anybody enlisting a complete stranger to join them in smuggling German Lugars out of the Soviet Union must be a con man, an idiot, or both.

I was glad that my backpack only had dirty laundry in it. I had no camera to steal. My dwindling money supply was securely around my waist. He was not scary. I actually found him entertaining. He and I decided to go out together and see what Munich is best known for, the beer hall.

All the Swedes in the room have been to a German beer hall. They know those places are as big as gymnasiums and they know what goes on there. None of them has gone twice. A beer hall is where people go to drink lots of beer.

One of the Swedes puts it very well, "Rude behavior happens all the time."

My Munich roommate and I went to the Hofbrau House, supposedly the biggest drinking establishment in the world. Inside, a thousand loud people packed the large hall. Heavyweight security guards with nightsticks patrolled the aisles. Serving women in low cut outfits with push-up bras brought liter size beer mugs out to the appreciative crowd. People sang German songs loudly, very loudly.

I was just looking around, enjoying a place unlike any place I had ever seen before. My roommate however, was coming up with a plan for us to steal our big beer mugs. He was telling me I should do it too, not to be afraid.

"Stealing the beer steins will be easy," he said. It was why he pushed me to take seats right next to the emergency exit.

"You're nuts!" I told him. "Does that big German guard standing between us and the door mean anything to you?"

My roommate said there are always fights in the beer hall. And whenever a fight happens, the guard always leaves the door. We could run out with the mugs then.

I told him I did not want to steal a mug.

Everything happened as he predicted. Men at a nearby table got into a fistfight. Whistles blew. Guards, including the one on the door rushed over. We and several other people near the door rushed out. He carried two beer mugs. Everybody else ran down the street. We walked back to the hotel.

He pushed hard to get me to take that second beer mug. He said it was a gift but I knew I would owe him for it.

He would not take no for an answer. I got tired of repeating myself so I stopped talking. Then I got tired of hearing him telling me what to do.

I am someone who does not take orders well.

I yelled at him. "Why the hell do I want to carry a big beer mug around Europe? It is heavy; it does not fit in my backpack, and I do not want to mail it home to my father. If you give me that beer mug, I will leave it at the hotel for the maid".

He did not understand my refusal to steal but he did understand me not wanting to carry it. He did not ask me to take the mug again. He stopped trying to get me to join his treasure hunt to the U.S.S.R.

When I woke up in the morning he was gone.

I end my story by telling the group the American said he was going to mail both mugs back to his father. His father would be impressed his son stole them. He said his family was rich and they had been rich for generations. After he made big bucks turning over the German Lugars his father and his uncles would be even more impressed.

"Do you think he was he a con-man?" I ask the teachers. I get unexpected comments from them.

"That is what is great about America: you can make a lot of money."

"And you get to keep it."

"Not like in Sweden."

Now I'm saying, "You all own cars; you take vacations. You told me you spend a lot on clothes. I think you're doing pretty well. In America, we think all Swedes are..." They interrupt me.

Several people are talking at once. People are sounding defensive or offended. They want bigger cars and vacations around the world. They are worried they will never have as much money as their parents. They might work all their lives and not be able to afford a second house in the mountains.

"We think all Swedes are..." but they interrupt me again. People talking blame the government and the Social Democratic party.

My friend, the den mother says, "Do you know in Sweden any six people can join together and form a club and get money from the government? You and five friends can form a photography club and get money to buy your equipment."

How would I know if that was true? People make up 89.5% of all facts and figures used in arguments. Then somebody else repeats the misinformation. It becomes true by repetition and the debate starts being about numbers.

I am not arguing facts and figures. This is about what is fair, or good for our countries.

These Swedish teachers hate taxes.

"But taxes pay your salaries," I say

I hear, "Not those taxes."

I finally get to say, "In America, we think all Swedes are rich."

One of the Swedish teachers, a man says, "But

the point is after taxes, I make only a few thousand kroners more than people who prepare food in the cafeteria."

A woman asks, "Is that true?"

I add, "Wages in the U.S. and Sweden are the envy of workers around the world."

He answers her question. "Yes, I asked them; it's true!" then he turns towards me, "Don't you understand, I went to the university; they didn't."

Am I <u>really</u> having a late night, college dorm bull session? Yes! And I'm in Sweden! It might be four against one, very bad odds for me but I am used to that. So I challenge him anyway. "Isn't being well off enough? Do you have to make a whole bunch more money than the next guy before you're happy?"

"Are you insulting him?" I hear.

"NO!" I feel the alcohol. We have all been drinking. I know *the System* wants working people to fight each other for bigger paychecks. When our focus is only on dividing the pie they give us, people compare their pay to the next guy's and feel worse off, not better. I say, "Life does not have to be a rat race."

Now he turns to everyone in the room. He is telling us how it is perfectly normal for people with a higher education to have a better life than people who did not go to the university. It was always that way. It is a "natural right."

"Natural right?" I question him hard. "Like the right of kings to free labor or the right of white men to hold slaves? They were also called natural rights not long ago. This is 1968; our countries are rich; people who work hard should be well paid. The good life does not need to be reserved for kings, thieves, and children with rich parents who can send their kids to college."

In an instant, I turn into an alien who lost his Universal Translator. Suddenly they are all talking, they're arguing, and I don't understand a word of it. Since my return from the shower, every single word spoken in this room has been in English. Now, that's over. Everyone is speaking Swedish.

I am the odd man out. But they are looking at me. I focus on a candle. And the clock next to it.

One minute goes by. My arguing got stupid. I forgot Sweden is a country that still has a king and they or their parents paid for their college education. Was I rude? I am a guest in their country, in her bedroom. Do not bite the hand that feeds you goes double here.

Two minutes go by. I think they are arguing about me, about what I said. I am in trouble. If they kick me out it is too late to get a room anywhere. Sleeping in the park is a completely bad option. People are talking loudly but not emphatically. No one is using their hands to say anything.

Then, in English, my Swedish friend uses a tone of voice that makes everyone stop and listen. She says, "Let's not talk in Swedish. Our American friend will think we are talking about him." I will never know. I am relieved at the return of communication and my Swedish friend's assistance.

They all are speaking English again. These people are more than just fluent; they use American slang. Most speak without Swedish accents.

I tell people how impressive their command of the English language is. "Are you all English teachers?"

"No."

"Sweden has the best schools in the world," someone says. "Everyone starts learning English in elementary school."

I do not say, great schools and high taxes probably go hand in hand but that is what I am thinking.

The party is now breaking up. One man just goes out the door. Two women shake my hand before leaving. I get a "Thanks for an interesting evening."

As the man I argued with the most leaves, he tells me, "The Social Democratic party will be defeated in the next election. They will never again hold power in Sweden."

I thank everybody for talking with me.

Finally, here just three of us are in the bedroom. The last man, the man who brought me the towel says, "You will go with me and sleep on the rug in my room."

I blurt out, "I want to sleep here."

He and my Swedish friend laugh, maybe at my voice or my naiveté. "No man sleeps here," he says.

In the morning, he and I wake up early and go down to the cafeteria for breakfast.

The food service workers have been working for an hour already and have prepared a feast for the students to eat. I hope the students appreciate it.

CHAPTER 6

MORE HITCHHIKING

This morning I am walking out of Malmo and the gear feels heavy on my back. The cold wet fog in Copenhagen yesterday is in Sweden today. Strangely, before I even get to the highway an old Volvo passes me and jerks hard towards the curb. I am not even hitchhiking yet but the driver turns and waves. I walk up, go to the driver's side window and get a surprise.

An elderly Swedish gentleman is the driver. He is alone and says, "Don't you want a ride? Get in." I sit down on a comfortable bench seat. His car is immaculate inside. The flannel upholstery is grey and the metal dashboard has chrome trim someone recently polished. The Volvo's body style dates it to the mid 1940's and he dates to about 1890.

The car smells good. I am at ease, heading north to Gothenburg with Ice on my mind. Then he gets my attention by telling me he hasn't done very much driving on the right hand side of the road.

The old man says, "Less than one year ago the entire country of Sweden switched from driving on the left hand side of the road to driving on the right." One morning every Swedish driver had something new to think about. The road rules changed from driving as they do in Great Britain to driving on the same side of the road as the rest of Europe.

This man has been driving on the left side his entire life. He's been staying on the left when making turns, stopping on the left at intersections, and sticking to the left to avoid head-on collisions. At the beginning of the changeover, he was not driving on the left or right. He waited for things to "settle down."

Today he is driving on the right side of the road and going north to visit family near Gothenburg. It's the first long trip he's taken since the change. I realize he needs me as much as I need him.

He asks me if I have any idea how difficult it is to hug the right side of the road after a lifetime of hugging the left side.

"No, I don't."

"Well it is. So if I am a bit off in my turns, forgive me."

I already know what he means.

In Malmo, there are new traffic signs reminding drivers of the correct side of the road. But when we leave town nothing aims drivers towards the right. His old habits return while turning corners. Too often he is swinging over into the left hand lane. After slowing down, he pulls back into the right hand lane.

I don't have to say anything. He talks to himself the entire time in Swedish. Then he apologizes every time in English.

Soon, city traffic disappears. Open space surrounds the car. The highway straightens out. Clean, new, black asphalt covers the road and a big yellow stripe down the middle separates the one lane in each direction. We both calm down.

My driver wants to tell me about how Sweden has changed. He talks about how people never had it so good. Then he says it again, and says more. Wages are good in Sweden. Everyone eats well. All children go to good schools. If they get sick, the doctor is free. I am getting an earful but I love it.

He talks. I listen. "Sweden used to be a poor country with some very rich families; now Sweden is a rich country." He says the change was the result of winning elections, not losing them.

There is no doubt he is a strong supporter of the Social Democratic Party. He gives me some advice about how people have to know what side to take. And they have to vote or, "The people's side never wins." He talks for a long time about all the good his political party has done for his country.

Eventually I get to ask him a question, to tell me the biggest change in Sweden in his lifetime.

The old man says, "When I was your age, most people never left their hometown their entire lives." They were too poor. Now ordinary Swedes travel anywhere they want to go.

He adds, "Young people these days only think about making money. When they start to think about each other, all of them will be better off."

Many older people have voluntarily given up their drivers' licenses because they might cause an accident and hurt somebody else. However, my driver still thinks changing the side of the road Swedes drive on was a good idea.

"This shows the world Sweden is a very strong united country," he says.

I cannot fathom what it would take for all the drivers in the U.S.A. to change the side of the road they drive on. The United States cannot even change to the metric system where all measurement is divisible by ten. We are the only big country in the world that still measures using sixteenths, 12, 3, and 5280.

The old man and I slowly drive by beautiful pastures and farmland. We see thousands of acres of dense forest. We look at the land through raindrops on the old Volvo's windshield. Nearly everything out there is green; the wetness turns all the green into super-saturated green. The wipers are making a comforting sound. We are going along quietly now. Sweden is beautiful. It reminds me of rural Pennsylvania.

I am glad we're not stuck behind a very slow moving farm vehicle, waiting for a break in oncoming traffic to pull out and pass. With this driver, passing anything would be dangerous. And I am glad no one is passing us at extremely high speeds; the other cars are zooming around us at only about 120 kmph.

My driver and this new side of the road thing have me anxious but so far, everything is OK.

I hear a siren, see flashing lights, and a car passes us with *POLIS* on the side. It's not for us; the highway patrol is pulling over the car that just passed us. The cops are driving a brand new Swedish Volvo.

Come to think of it. The German police drove German BMW's, the Italian police drove Italian Fiats, the Czechoslovakian police drove a car I never heard of, and the French drove very big French Citroens. However, the big, black word on the side of their cruisers was always the same word, *POLIZEI* (Ger.), *POLIZIA* (It.), *POLICIE* (Cz.), and *POLICE* (Fr.).

As I hitchhiked around, the police frequently slowed down, looked me over, and drove on by (except in Germany and Monaco.)

European police cars are all painted the same, mostly white like cop cars back home. And policemen's jobs are the same as in the U.S. too.

My driver slows down. He says he will make a right-hand turn at the next intersection. Gothenburg is about 25 kilometers straight ahead. I am glad the rain has stopped.

We have been driving together for at least two enjoyable hours. I give him my thanks for the ride and the interesting conversation. I tell him his old car is cool and he did a fine job driving on the right.

I get out. Tall pine trees surround me. I am at an intersection of the highway and a local road where the old Volvo turned. There are just one or two cars per minute speeding by. Speeding is bad, frequency good.

I know what to do. I stand in a spot very visible to drivers going north and pull a sign out of my backpack. It is a large piece of white cardboard with a big black arrow on it. I hold it out. It is easier to see than my thumb. I know a car will stop for me eventually, but when? I hope I won't be late.

If I am late for my date with Ice, I will just call and see her tomorrow. She will understand. What am I thinking; I don't even know if she will be waiting for me at all. Am I going to be stood up after all this hitchhiking?

Waiting gives me time for reflection. Funny how life works out, there are things you do at the start of something you never want to do again. Getting to Gothenburg in a car would take 20 minutes. Walking there would take about six hours and I would hurt my back again carrying the backpack and bedroll. I have learned to wait for my ride, not walk.

Life can also give you experiences later that would have defeated you at the beginning. If I have to wait all day for a ride, it will not be the first time. Earlier in my trip, when I entered Italy I waited over seven hours in the same spot and almost gave up hitchhiking. I almost bought a Eur-rail pass for $100.

I think most American students in Europe bought rail passes. The story of my trip after Nice would have been just like theirs if I had bought that rail pass in Italy.

Italy introduced me to long waits. Thousands of young hitchhikers from all around the world were on the roads there. It was common to see two dozen people hitchhiking at a major intersection or fifty spread out around a highway on-ramp. But I didn't see that at first.

I woke up alive in the Italian motel where I

rented a room with a stranger. Everything was fine. We got coffee and rolls for breakfast. Then we drove south. He was a good man, some kind of engineer.

When we got to Genoa, he started down the entrance ramp for the auto-strada. But since he was traveling west to Milan, and I was going south to Rome he pulled over and let me out.

The Italian Auto-strada is a modern, multi-lane, limited access, divided highway. Two cross Italy, one from side to side and the other from top to bottom. Drivers have to pay money at tollbooths to use it.

I was waiting near a dozen lanes of traffic at the toll plaza in a rocky ravine. It was rush hour and the toll takers and ticket givers were very busy.

I wrote *SUD – ROMA* with crayon in large letters on a white piece of cardboard. I held up my sign and stuck out my thumb. I was with approximately twenty other people also trying to get rides.

I did not get a ride. One hour spent hitchhiking became two. Other hitchhikers got rides, I didn't. Maybe I was in the wrong spot. I moved further up the entrance ramp. It did not help. I moved even closer to the main road. It was getting hot and I was still waiting.

Two hours became three. The traffic was far less than earlier. Every person who started on the entrance ramp with me in the morning was gone.

Many more people arrived and left and I was still standing.

Three hours spent hitchhiking became four, then five. I stopped counting sports cars with their tops down. I grew tired of looking at drivers. At midday it was hot, and I was the only person hitchhiking on the ramp. I was still striking out.

I walked away, and walked twenty minutes down the main road before I got to a restaurant. With my backpack and bedroll, it was obvious to everyone a hitchhiker just came in.

I sat at the counter. No one spoke English to me. I just pointed to some kind of sandwich on the menu and ordered it. I cashed a five-dollar travelers check. The lunch cost thirty-five cents.

I had spent over half the day in one spot. It was now impossible to get to Rome before dark.

I thought about buying a train ticket to Rome. Then I thought about giving up completely on hitchhiking and getting a Eur-rail pass. I could travel all over Europe by train in the company of other students.

A Eur-rail pass had its pro's and con's. Before the trip began I considered it, and rejected it but the pass was more appealing to me than waiting.

Eating provided energy for my spirit and sitting helped my feet feel better. I reminded myself that I knew everyday was not going to be an easy day. Even if I stood watching cars drive by for an entire day, it was still more interesting than what I did last summer.

That was when I stood next to a big injection-molding machine all day. I pulled plastic radio knobs out of a hot mold, cut off the excess plastic, and got ready for the mold to open again so I could repeat the task.

I was a plastic injection molding machine operator. It helped pay for college and a little fun. And I learned a lot. Some of the other operators had worked there for years. They told me the pay was ok, the boss fair, and the factory a decent place to work.

As a summer worker I was paid $1.60 an hour, the minimum wage in the United States. I thought I would do what I wanted with my paycheck. Going to the movies cost one dollar. For $1.69, I could buy a T-bone steak dinner with a baked potato and vegetables at Tad's steaks. For 1000 hours labor I could get a brand new Volkswagen Beetle ($1,600.) In 1968, American workers were just about the best-paid workers on the planet Earth.

As it turned out, I worked a lot of overtime. I spent most of my time in the factory and very little of it having fun. But here I am in Europe with money I didn't spend last summer.

1968 and I'm Hitchhiking Through Europe

I was in the open air. I had the chance for an adventure. I was in a foreign place I would never see again and I wasn't working. I could walk around, eat when I felt like it, or do something else if I pleased.

I decided it was time to do something else. I went to the restroom, took off my cut-off jeans and put on heavyweight navy blue cotton long pants; so what if it was hot outside. I took off the T-shirt and put on a light blue, short sleeved, Oxford cloth shirt with a button down collar. I took off my sandals and put on shoes.

And I made a second decision. I would go wherever the first car that stopped for me was going.

I walked backwards and hitchhiked along the main road to the entrance of the super-highway. No ride yet. I got to the entrance ramp. I stood up real straight and put my backpack and bedroll behind me.

It was now the middle of the afternoon. Two more hours went by. Traffic increased. New hitchhikers arrived and left. I was still hitchhiking and not winning the pick-up lottery.

I started to think about what was in Genoa for me to see. Christopher Columbus was born in Genoa. That was when a young man driving a red Alfa Romeo stopped for me. Before I even asked him where he was going, I got in. Imagine my feelings when he said "Milan." I could have been in Milan this morning!

His Alfa was soon flying down the auto-strada. I could see his speedometer's needle pointing to 160, 170, 185, then 200 kmph. There is something about young men and speed. Whenever we looked at each other, we were both smiling.

Within an hour, highway signs were announcing turn off here for Milan. This was long before I expected it. But he was not turning. We shot past the Milan exit. He was going to a suburb of Milan.

Next were highway signs in Italian reading, "Road to Rome 5Km, Road to Florence, 5Km" and they had arrows pointing to the right.

"Exito, exito, Roma, Roma" I said, pointing to the large road signs.

He immediately pulled over. I got out and thanked him. I was very grateful he picked me up but not about where he left me off.

I was walking along the narrow shoulder of the super-highway, which is illegal. Cars were zooming by me at high speed, which was dangerous. I was thinking about being on the ring road around a major city, which every hitchhiker knows is bad. I was looking down the ramp to the toll plaza and at least twenty people were there, trying to get rides up to here.

All of a sudden, a large Italian sedan stopped right in front of me. For me!

A woman, from the front passenger seat jumped out and quickly opened the trunk and back door. She was urgent. I threw my stuff into the trunk and was fast inside. I sat down next to two children around ten years old, a girl and a boy.

"Graci" is the Italian word for thanks and I said it several times as we pulled onto to the auto-strada.

The windows were up; the air-conditioning was on; the children looked at me. I smiled at them. The woman said something in Italian to the man driving and then he twisted his head around, reached back and shook my hand. He said, in Italian accented English "You are welcome."

What kind of people pull over on a super-highway and pick up a hitchhiker who is not even requesting a ride? They looked normal. The man and woman talked to one another without anger. Their children seemed comfortable. One read a comic book; the other watched where we were going.

The driver asked about my destination. I just said "south" because he had just taken the exit for the southbound auto-strada.

"Have you been to Florence yet?" he asked me.
"No."

"Then you will come to Florence with us," he said. "Florence is our city."

Florence was closer than Rome and we would

get there before nightfall. It is an important city. Of course I would go. Florence, how could I have forgotten about Florence?

I leaned forward and told him I would love to visit his city. I told him about where I was from, about being a student, and started to talk about the places I had visited so far and about Spain.

He asked no questions. I stopped talking. The woman turned, touched her children and smiled at us. Everybody was quiet. I became quiet like everyone else and just watched the scenery go by. We went over some mountains and then through a tunnel underneath mountains.

Twenty-four hours ago, I had been in Southern France; now I am in Central Italy. Yesterday's dinner, the hotel room, breakfast, and lunch all combined had cost less than three dollars. I spent zero for transportation. I was living the hitchhiker's life.

As the sun went down, we pulled into the rest area on the auto-strada for dinner. The five of us walked across a big pedestrian bridge from the parking lot to the restaurant on the other side of the highway. While cars were speeding underneath our feet, he asked if I had lira to spend for dinner. I did not need him to buy me dinner. He said he wasn't offering to. The restaurant only took lira. No other currencies were accepted.

I said, "Yes, I have lira." My five dollars converted into thousands of lira.

As we were walking, he also brought up where to sleep that night. Their apartment was too small for an overnight guest. He talked about an old farmhouse on the outskirts of Florence recently converted into a beautiful youth hostel. Acres of farmland surrounded the place. I could stay there. He would drive me to the front door; it was not far.

Over dinner, he talked about how he and his wife hitchhiked all over Italy when they were college students. Every summer they got rides from strangers to ancient ruins. They camped in Italy's National Parks and slept on her beaches.

They loved Italy. He said Italian people were wonderful. Back in those days, they had no money and people gave them rides everywhere. He said that was why they pick up hitchhikers now, especially hitchhikers in trouble. They were the kind of people who return favors once provided to them.

These people were wonderful people. And their children were beautiful children.

I was with them for almost four hours. It was the most peaceful ride I had all summer. When I got out at the farmhouse-hostel, it was dark. This was another time I could not thank people enough for the ride they gave me, and I told them.

More Hitchhiking

I told myself the day spent waiting at the Genoa tollbooths ended very well.

However, I did not sleep in the old farmhouse youth hostel. As the big sedan pulled away, I saw twenty young people standing outside the entrance. They told me the hostel was filled up. None of us could stay there. Everyone was waiting for someone to decide what to do next. A few wanted to take the very long walk back into town and find another place to stay. Some talked about everyone sleeping in the nearby field.

I was up for sleeping in a field in Italy. Back home I had slept in fields plenty of times. I wanted to know what kind of field they were talking about. Was it one with cow manure, raw earth, or growing vegetables?

Enough waiting, we all went and looked at the field. It was pastureland but did not smell. Most people stayed. We put down our stuff, sat around and talked. Eventually we rolled out our bags and went to sleep. In the morning we faced a bigger problem than cows.

A girl discovered her camera was missing. Histrionics and acrimony got our blood flowing instead of a campfire.

A big American the size of a football player instantly accused two dark skinned North Africans of stealing it. He said we should search their bags. Then somebody else, a little guy with a Long Island accent said somebody who makes that kind of accusation should allow us to search his bag first, and then everybody should open their bag for a search.

"No I won't!" and "Go to hell!" were people's responses.

Somebody tried to play detective among the dozen of us. Next, we tried to prevent a fistfight. There was pushing and shoving and yelling. The situation was going from bad to worse real fast and all the tears and anger happened while the wet morning dew covered us all; while everyone was cold and before any coffee.

Nothing was resolved. People just stopped paying attention and the group dissolved while the girl was still crying and camera-less. She stayed with the football player. I felt sorry for her.

After that sour start to the day, I went into the farmhouse youth hostel and reserved a bed for that night. The place was not heated. There was no coffee there and nothing to eat. However, the place had real beds. People did not have to sleep on the floor.

To get warm and to stop being hungry, I walked to a restaurant on the road to Florence. I got a hot "Americano" breakfast to eat and then went into the city to see the sights.

By chance, I ran into one of the young North African men. He said he was in Italy to attend college in Rome. He told me his dad was a doctor back in Tunis, the capital of Tunisia. We walked around together. He practiced his English and was interesting company because he knew a lot about the Italian Renaissance.

Florence was the city-state that ruled central Italy 500 years ago when Rome was a poor town. Machiavelli, who wrote the book about how to stay in power was from Florence. Leonardo da Vinci and Michelangelo worked there. The city is filled with magnificent public artwork.

During the day, Florence did not disappoint. The people were enjoyment for the eyes. So were the outdoor statues, museums, and old buildings.

We visited the Duomo, an old black and white cathedral in the center of town. I mean the exterior walls had wide, horizontal stripes of white marble and black marble. It was cold inside and I could smell hundreds of votive candles burning.

Michelangelo's statue of David was outdoors across from the cathedral. This is the David who slew Goliath in the Bible story. The sculpture is over 300 years old, 15 feet tall, and very realistic. David stands proudly naked (without a fig leaf) and within sight of the church's front door. How great is that!

We visited the Uffizi Palace and saw paintings by the masters. A dirty old painting by Hieronymus Bosch caught my eye. I remembered it from an art history book. It was really dirty; I could barely make out details here that had been easy to see in the book.

My Tunisian friend and I never discussed our morning in the field. After good Italian food for dinner, we both headed back to the hostel. But no one can reserve their night in a hostel. We found our bags in a big pile outside the place.

I went in and put up an argument; wanted my dollar back. The evening clerk said he did not know anything about reservations. There was no one else to complain to and nowhere else to get a cheap room. It was late.

I did not want to sleep in that field again. It was too big a bad memory. My Tunisian friend and I walked back into the center of Florence. Near the Duomo, we found fortress walls with an open gate leading to a large courtyard and several government buildings. No one was around. We slept on a porch so filthy the building may have been vacant.

In the morning, I noticed my sleeping bag and I had turned brown. Public facilities for hitchhikers provided by the City of Florence helped us clean up. My bag stayed damp and covered with dirt.

Immediately after breakfast, I started

hitchhiking to Rome. I stood at the entrance to the Italian Auto-strada with dozens of other people, including men in suits and elderly couples. I thought I would have to wait a long time.

I did not. Two men in a sports car with the top down picked me up. I squeezed myself into the wooden, carpeted, passenger "back seat" and was immediately uncomfortable. It was an awful seat but it was my ride to Rome!

I leaned forward and the Italian men in front gave me advice, "Try your luck with English girls, Swedish girls, and German girls. Not the Italian girls, they are no fun."

These were middle-aged men and they talked a lot about girls. I listened to them and to the loud rattling of ball bearings in the gearbox. Fifth gear was shot. The driver started using fourth gear for highway cruising.

"One day I will have to get that fixed," the driver yelled over all the noise.

That day was coming soon. As we entered Rome, he could not get the car into fifth or fourth gears. We traveled in third gear.

The driver said he would do me a favor. He would take me to the best woman for me in all Rome.

I needed to know more. He said she ran a pensione, a place to get a nice room for the night. It would not be expensive. She would be happy to see me. I would do it.

We entered Rome through a gate in brick walls built almost two thousand years ago around the entire city. The driver yelled, "A new building in Rome is one built in the last three hundred years."

Majestic trees lined wide boulevards. I saw people walking everywhere. Some Romans looked at us in this little sports car, making a big racket as we accelerated after each stoplight. The city was great to drive around in, even though I had been stuffed into that awful back seat for way too long.

When we finally stopped at the pensione, both the driver and his friend had to pry me out. One man rang the bell. A woman came to the door and the driver spoke with her in Italian. Maybe he gave her some money; I couldn't tell for sure.

For me, she was the best woman in all Rome. She was my mother's age. She fed me some lunch and then we went upstairs. My room overlooked a piazza, Italian for a public square in the city. The room had white curtains, a circular braided rug, an old wooden chest of drawers with a lace doily on it, and a super soft bed. It smelled great. The bathroom was down the hall.

She watched me unpack my bag and suggested I take a bath before going out. My skin was oily from the windswept, two and a half hour car ride plus too many days sleeping outdoors. A bath was a great idea.

I went to the Roman Forum. The cobblestone streets where Julius Caesar walked were still there for me to walk on. I saw the foundation of the House of the Vestal Virgins. I passed through a giant triumphal arch built two thousand years ago to commemorate the Roman conquest of Jerusalem. Carved in stone on its side was a procession with men carrying a large Jewish menorah. I was impressed with how much of ancient Rome still exists for people to see.

I went to the Vatican and visited Saint Peter's Basilica. The choir singing, incense burning, colored light streaming through stained glass windows, and cold marble columns touched my senses. Downstairs there were supposed to be crypts with bones of saints on display. However, all the steps were either closed off or guarded. I guess we were not allowed down there.

After dinner, I went back to the pensione. All my clothes lay on the bed, clean. I was so surprised; I did not even notice that my sleeping bag was gone. Cost for the night: $2.30. { I know the exact amount because I wrote it on a postcard I sent my grandmother from Rome. She kept it on her dresser until she died in 1981. An aunt of mine saved it and gave it to me.}

In the morning, the owner invited me into her kitchen. She set out breakfast and we talked some more. She mentioned washing my sleeping bag. That was a great surprise. She also said she loved many U.S. soldiers. She surprised me further by asking this: "Maybe your father?"

"During the war my father worked in a factory making artillery shells." I always gave straight answers.

I saw this woman every morning. She suggested ancient ruins I should visit and neighborhoods to find good, cheap restaurants. I walked wherever I wanted and wandered around Rome each day.

One afternoon, I found the ancient Pantheon. It was amazing inside. I think it would have been an ambitious construction project even if workers built it last year instead of in 181 AD. I thought about Jim.

Then I found a big pyramid! It must have been one hundred feet high. The surface was a smooth white stone. The old red brick city walls touched both sides of the gleaming pyramid. No sign explained why this giant thing was stuck in the wall and there was no one around to ask.

I walked on a path alongside the wall. Slowly the path rose and then I was walking on top of the old city walls of Rome. The wall was along the crest of a hill. I could see miles away. I was all alone and the bricks were loosening under my steps. The edge of the wall fell apart and the bricks slid to the ground!

Embarrassed, I looked around. No one saw this. There were no signs around to tell people to stay off the walls. In addition, many "new" buildings nearby were built with the same bricks as the walls. There was no doubt where the builders got the bricks for construction.

For dinner, I found a restaurant smaller than a two-car garage. It was packed and I got the last empty seat. Several Italian sailors in uniform were there with dates. These were beautiful women and they were revealing a lot in their low cut dresses. People were all singing and laughing as they ate and drank. Everybody was having a great time. Ah, la dolce vita!

The menu was only in Italian. Every other person in the place was Italian. By accident, I picked a delicious meal of tripe, pasta with a white sauce, bread and wine. The meal and an evening's entertainment cost less than a dollar.

I thanked my Italian friend the next morning for sending me in that direction and stayed at her pensione for three days. I think I was her only guest.

When I left, I told her about all the Italians who helped me get to Rome: the engineer who shared a motel room with me, the smiling young man in his speeding Alfa Romeo, the wonderful young couple with two children, and the two men in the sports car who knocked on her door. She told me she didn't know any of them.

A hitchhiker knows rides can take a full day of waiting or rides can come before they are asked for. I'm hitchhiking through Europe getting both kinds of rides and every kind of ride in between.

Now I'm in Sweden waiting for a ride into Gothenburg. Any car will do. Is Ice going to be there at the end of my journey?

A man in a Saab picks me up and drops me off a little early in the center of town.

I call Ice's house. No one answers. Maybe no one is home from work yet. "Why did I call? I have her address. She expects me at five. I should just sit on a park bench and wait." I am so nervous I am talking to myself.

What did she mean telling me to ask anyone for directions to her street? Whatever she meant, I am very glad I made it this far. I think she will be there for me. The time does not pass by quickly.

I feel days go by before time comes to get off the bench and ask for directions. I show the address to a man who looks like a local. He does not speak English but understands what I want. He takes me over to the bus stop, points to the map there, and traces with his finger from where we are to her street. Her house is on the main road. One bus starts here and goes there. What could be easier?

I say "tax" to the man. I do not know how the word is spelled but saying it in Sweden is saying "thanks."

Waiting for a bus to Ice's house is not like hitchhiking. Buses in Europe run frequently, like the subways and trains. I am sure a bus will be picking me up here soon. But it takes forever.

I see it coming. I am on the bus and now even more nervous. Is she really going to be there or will my trip of a thousand km end with me being stood up?

CHAPTER 7

ICE

People coming home from work fill the bus going to Ice's house. Everyone dresses so well. Most men have on suits and ties; the women wear cotton dresses. Some passengers carry light sweaters.

I carry my backpack and bedroll. Jeans and a slightly wrinkled cotton shirt have been my uniform all summer. I stand out in the crowd but no one seems to be paying any notice.

I am worrying; there is no use denying it. I'm keeping my eyes on where we're going and keeping my mind off Ice.

The bus gets out of downtown. We turn onto a wide street with small businesses on it. On some blocks, tall trees and open fields line both sides. We are going uphill. People are walking on the sidewalk. There is a billboard. And red cars. Have I seen this place before? Am I having deja vue?

Right now, I am so nervous I'm sweating. Nearby are some mountains. Thick clouds are breaking up on them. The sun is shining through the clouds behind me. After all that dreary weather, today will turn out to be a beautiful day.

We enter a residential area. The bus takes us past big houses; most of them are white; they have red tile roofs, short driveways, and garages. Each house has a small front yard and is close to the next house. I see big backyards with tall trees. This is a nice neighborhood. We are on Ice's street.

I am counting house numbers. We are approaching her block. I'm off the bus and can see her waiting outside. My feet are carrying me across the street, over the sidewalk, and up her driveway. She's really there. This is GREAT!

An older man is waiting too. He is behind the car. Before I say anything more than "hi," Ice is over to me and kisses me on the cheek. She looks older without her cousin standing next to her. We quick-hug. She looks beautiful.

The man does not come over to our side of the car. He asks her from that distance, in English, where she is going.

I hear myself say "hi" to him. I guess he is her father but he's saying nothing to me. I start walking towards him but Ice holds my sleeve, restraining me.

Ice tells him we are going to the Chinese restaurant in town, and she will take me to the cabins in the park to sleep. She won't be back late; she has to work tomorrow.

One minute later, I am waiting for the bus again but this time Ice is standing with me. I am in Sweden, have just picked up a man's daughter for a date, and he didn't even say hello to me. And her restraining me, what was that about? Did something strange happen or was it just something I didn't understand?

Ice and I are not affectionate. We are not holding hands or anything. She is talking, and smiling. We're both smiling. I'm feeling the sun's rays warming me as the damp day disappears. We get on the bus. Ice asks what I think of Sweden.

"Since I arrived yesterday all the Swedes I talked to were friendly and very smart, and your country is very beautiful." This must have been the right thing to say.

Ice takes my hands and says she is excited about my visit; "A boy I met on my vacation hitchhiked all the up to Sweden to see me." (Boy?)

After I telephoned her, Ice said she called her

cousin Marie, who was jealous, very jealous. Our need to get off the bus interrupts the rest of whatever she was going to say.

We get off but we are not even half way to the center of town. The bus has stopped at a dirt road leading into a large park. We begin to walk towards the trees. This is not an urban park.

When the dirt road reaches the trees and goes around a bend, we have left the city behind us. We are in a forest.

We walk for a while until we come upon a clearing. There are several small wooden cabins arranged in a circle. Ice calls out. No one answers. She explains the campsite is free overnight housing for people who are hiking in the forest.

She says, "No one is here."

Ice encourages me to pick a cabin; I do. I go inside while she waits outside. The cabin is clean. Its rough-cut pine exterior walls are also its interior walls. The large window openings have screens, no glass. There are four hard wooden platform beds and my gear goes on one. There is a small table and no chairs. A few shelves are attached to the wall. The toilet and shower are somewhere else. I am sure they are outdoors.

"Can I just leave my stuff here?" I yell.

Ice comes to the screen door and looks in. She

clamps her hands over her brow to see better. Her body makes a big shadow on the screen. "You should claim your bed now," she says. "When we get back the place might be filled with campers."

She looks great as a shadow.

I ask, "I mean is it safe?"

"No one is going to steal your stuff," she says with a laugh. I like her laugh.

I unroll my sleeping bag. Someone would have to be crazy or desperate to want it. The thing smells of too many nights use. Too many times sleeping on the earth.

Rome was the last time my bag was washed and I stayed in the pensione over a month ago. I am in Sweden, remembering Rome and the woman who loved Americans. I want to tell Ice about how good that woman was to me.

I was having a trip where people were taking good care of me most of the time and ignoring me, or worse, just a little bit of the time. That is OK.

Ice is definitely in the "taking good care of me" category. We leave the camp. She knows a trail from the cabins to the center of town. At times, the path goes down steeply. I could not do this carrying the backpack and bedroll. I am so glad I left my stuff at the cabins and absolutely thrilled to be hiking in Sweden with Ice.

Occasionally, we see the low sun through the trees. We sit on a big boulder to rest. Soon the sun has set. It is getting dark fast.

This is Ice's home turf. She grew up here and knows the trail well. Dark doesn't matter. Besides, she brought a flashlight in her handbag. She shines it upon tree roots, rocks, and crevices to avoid. The hike could have been a disaster without her flashlight. Soon I see streetlights ahead of us. The trail drops us into the center of Gothenburg just as the evening sky turns black. We made it!

We see few other people around. There are not many cars on the street. About a football field away is a large imposing stone building. It is all lit up in a very dramatic fashion with spotlights on the columns.

"That is an example of Swedish Fascist Architecture," Ice says without a hint of judgment, pro or con. She talks about Swedish-German connections during World War 2 and says no one here apologizes for them. The Swedish government allowed Hitler to send troops through Sweden to occupy Norway. Swedish mines supplied iron ore to Germany for the entire war. People call the Swedish police the "Gestapo."

Maybe her father enjoys this Swedish Nationalism and does not want Ice out on a date with a foreigner.

"Do not break the law in Sweden," she warns. "You can be put in jail for a long time." She says this with a laugh, as if she would never be accused of breaking the law. After she laughs, I begin to hear her Swedish accent. Her voice takes my breath away.

Ice takes me into Gothenburg's comfortable, uncrowded, Chinese restaurant. At our table I listen to Ice talk. She likes this town and loves Sweden. However, she admits not having much experience living in other cities or other countries.

I start telling Ice about something I saw after leaving Prague that affected me deeply. I went to the Dauchau Concentration Camp near Munich, Germany. I became upset there. Sharing it with someone will help me feel better.

Ice does not want to hear about Dauchau. She asks if I had any trouble getting up to Sweden to see her. I think, "Just what trouble should I tell her about?"

"In Germany," I tell Ice. "I got stuck in one place longer than any in other place so far." It was after an early morning ride dropped me off at a very isolated exit of the German Autobahn. Acres of scrawny trees and weeds surrounded me. Nothing was nearby, no restaurant, no gas station or store, no farms or houses, not even any shade.

According to my map, the closest town was

twenty kilometers away, a five-hour walk. It was in a direction I did not want to go. Cars came by at the rate of two or three an hour.

I spent the entire day there. I drank my soda early. I ate all the candy and fruit I packed with me for emergencies like this.

Then the sun got very bright. Hours went by. I got very thirsty. I got hungry. The day became very hot. I stood up for each approaching car. I sat down. I even lay down. I walked down the on ramp to the autobahn. Speeding drivers blew their horns at me.

I remembered the week in jail penalty for hitchhiking on the autobahn. Students spread that rumor in every youth hostel in Europe and after seeing the hitchhiker taken away by the German highway police the previous week, I was not taking a chance. I walked back up the on ramp.

I tell Ice there was nothing I could do except wait. I looked at the plants all around me. They were weeds. Some bristled with thorny seedpods. Nothing alive around me had been trimmed, cut or pruned. This landscape looked bombed-out and abandoned.

More hours went by. The soil was very coarse, yellow, and sandy. The sun was broiling me. I was too hot to think. It was too late to reach the town. I never thought about heatstroke. I was not feeling scared. It was daytime. I had survived a far worst spot in

Germany. I knew someone would pick me up eventually. After more than eight hours waiting someone did.

Ice tells me she never hitchhiked anywhere. She likes to fly. The airlines treat passengers like royalty with comfortable seats, good food, and very good hospitality. She also likes to travel by train. She asks me, "Did you ever travel around Europe any other way besides hitchhiking?"

"Back in Italy," I tell her, "I left Rome by train."

"Why?" is her next question.

"In Rome, hundreds of people were waiting for rides along the highway going north. Several hitchhikers told me they had been there a couple of days and not gotten a ride." I had even heard when drivers stopped, people mobbed them; there had been fistfights.

Standing next to a highway all day or for several days was not something I wanted to risk. And the scene was bad. So I went to the Rome train station and checked out ticket prices to other cities.

In Italy, my expenses were always under my $6 per day budget. I had enough surplus Italian lira to afford a second-class ticket all the way to Venice on the overnight train.

I left Rome that evening and sat down with some young Italians. We shared two long bench seats facing one another. We began talking as soon as I sat down. They were architectural graduate students.

When I told them what university I went to, they asked about an obscure building on my campus. Turns out it was the signature building of Louis Kahn, the architect and they loved Louis Kahn. I told them about the woods and pond at the building's base, and how it was a destination for lovers at night. That was a surprise to them.

One of the graduate students was a woman. The man sitting next to me whispered, "You should ask her for a date." He said she liked Americans.

While I talked, she kept looking at me and smiling. He kept telling me I should do it. I kept quiet. His volume increased and everyone could hear what we were discussing. I was put on the spot. Would I be insulting her by openly rejecting a chance to go out with her?

She turned, looked at me again and I asked, "When we get to Venice tomorrow morning, would you like to have breakfast with me?"

A firm "no" was her answer. She laughed. I laughed. Everyone had a good laugh.

I told Ice the train ride to Venice was a great break from hitchhiking. I loved traveling by train. The Italian students and I talked about cities and women far into the night. Then we fell asleep sitting up, even putting our heads on one another's shoulders. We woke up at the Venice train station and said good-bye.

In Venice, I saw Ice and Marie for the first time while we were taking the tour of the Ducal Palace. I moved close to them as the group moved from room to room. I introduced myself. I told them I was hitchhiking through Europe. I asked them what they thought of the palace.

The Chinese waiter comes to our table; Ice and I order. Then she takes my hand and says she and Marie met their hitchhiker in Venice, then met me again in Vienna, and then met me again in Prague. She says our coming together is fate.I loved her touch but I am not so sure about the hand of fate having anything to do with it.

In Venice, when we were walking around together Ice told me they were taking the train to Vienna the next day. Vienna is the capital of Austria and was already on my list of cities to visit. The two Swedish girls gave me an even better reason to go.

I started hitchhiking north when Ice and Marie left Venice. On the first day, I easily hitchhiked one long ride after another until lunchtime. Then the road started climbing hills. The weather changed from sunny and warm to gray clouds and colder temperatures. My ride took me up and over high mountain passes.

I was crossing the Dolomite Mountains of Northern Italy. Few cars were on the highway. There were long waits between each ride. I spent hours at high altitudes standing alongside mountains covered with loose rocks. The landscape was bleak and barren.

I grew up near mountains covered with forests hiding beautiful farms in their valleys. Nothing grew on these mountains. I saw no farms growing food, no animals grazing. From the road I saw only rocks, dirt, and fast moving creeks of black water. "What happened to all the trees?" I was thinking. Hitchhiking through the Dolomites became depressing.

A monk riding a motorcycle and wearing a thick brown robe stopped for me. When I hung on tight around sharp turns, he reminded me of my hippie-biker roommate David, who bathed monthly.

I came down a mountain hugging this stinking monk and his speeding motorcycle, and I froze my hands and butt off. When the main road turned north towards Austria, he invited me east to his monastery in Slovenia. He smiled and his eyes actually twinkled; maybe it was the cold, windy ride.

I started to tell him about Ice and Marie, and he interrupted me. He said he knew my answer already. I went north. I have always been curious about where the road east may have taken me.

Not to Ice and Marie.

My priority was to get up to Vienna quickly. I kept on hitchhiking into the evening.

That night I crossed the Austrian border and slept behind a gas station. It actually was a clean place to roll out my sleeping bag. It did not smell of gas or oil.

The next morning the sun woke me up. Its rays warmed my body. I felt good, challenged by the journey ahead, and strong. I rolled up my bag and started hitchhiking north again. I took only one day longer to get to Vienna than the two girls traveling on the train.

Tourists go to all the tourist places so I went to the giant Kunsthistorisches Museum and found Ice and Marie there. The two tall blondes were impossible to miss. I went right over to them. They were surprised to see me, and glad.

The three of us walked around the museum and saw great paintings two stories tall. We climbed giant Lion sculptures in the park. We spent the rest of the day just having fun.

I suggested we have dinner together. My idea was the restaurant a student had taken me to for breakfast. The meal was excellent and the pastries terrific. It was a subsidized cafeteria for people on limited incomes. The recently elected Austrian government started them all over the country to end hunger. The customers were retired people and students. I said we could go back to that one. Ice said she was ready.

Marie said it was not appropriate for them to go there. She inquired about my income. I told her it was strictly limited. I started out with $330 and now had half that much. But they wanted to know if my parents were rich. "I don't know how much money they have; it isn't my money." All our relatives seemed to live pretty well.

I knew what poor was. I grew up right outside of Trenton, New Jersey. Just a few blocks from our house families lived in run-down houses and three room shacks. At school, I had friends who felt embarrassed about wearing second hand clothing. Some kids could not even bring in three cents for milk. (We all chipped in and everyone drank milk.) Nobody talked about being on welfare but I know many children survived on it.

My father's factory job provided a nice house, two cars, plenty of all we needed and most of whatever we wanted. Until we were older, my mom worked at home taking good care of him, my sisters, and me. Were we rich?

I grew up thinking the American upper class consisted of doctors and lawyers. Then I met the children of the real upper class in college. I got a scholarship to an Ivy League university. In my classes, I met bored young men from families listed in the *Social Register*. During their entire lives, they would never have to do a day's work. (Is that necessarily richer?)

In 1968, the United States and Sweden competed for the top spot on the list of countries with the world's highest per worker income (not the world's richest person.) However, the two blondes might be too class conscious. They were also too nice and too good-looking for their direct questions to bother me. People should be direct. It is better than being vague, sarcastic, or telling lies. If my answers didn't bother them, so much the better. The three of us continued to enjoy Vienna until the sun was setting.

Before we parted, Ice, Marie, and I made plans to meet again in Prague, in Wenceslas Square, at noon in four days. I knew I could get there without a problem.

I got an early start out of Vienna. In the hot summer, early can be the best time of day. That morning the sky was a beautiful blue, the air cool and crisp; the strong low sunlight revealed textures everywhere. I decided to hike as far as I could. It was so nice I had the idea of hiking from the hostel all the way to the border with Czechoslovakia. It would take three days.

The wide Danube River is on the edge of Vienna. The bridge over it is long and flat. I walked across the Danube, over an island, then over the river again, then more islands. At the end of the bridge, I saw some woods not a town. The sun was hot.

I was walking north towards "Eastern Europe." I would be crossing the "iron curtain," exiting the "free world." I was heading for the "red menace." I was planning to take my chances inside the "communist block." {Czechoslovakia was part of the "evil empire" of the 1980's.} I wanted to see for myself what people living under communism were like.

Soon I stopped walking, turned, and looked at traffic. A car stopped immediately. All day I got one ride after another. My ride to the border was an elderly Austrian man driving his little granddaughter to the ballet. He said he picked me up because he wanted to and he went out of his way to show her the tank traps.

I sit in the restaurant and silently thank all those drivers who desired some company, needed to talk, or just wanted to help a stranger. So much for fate bringing Ice and me together three times. But I am not contradicting her about this tonight. Let her think our fate was to meet again and again. I like the fact she has been holding my hand for several minutes.

Our Chinese food arrives. Everything smells delicious and I am very hungry. We share.

Ice wants to know what I did after Prague. I want to know what she did after the Czech police took her and her cousin away in the black Mercedes-Benz.

Ice says the police asked them the question, "Who were those two boys?" They were asked this repeatedly and kept telling the police, "We just met them," and "We don't know who they are."

"Why didn't you just tell them the truth about an American hitchhiker and a Czech med student?" I asked. At first, Ice's face told me she did not like my question. Then she smiled.

The cops drove them around Prague slowly. It seemed like they were in the car for a long time. Eventually, the police stopped at their hotel. Ice says Marie was scared but she was never afraid. It all worked out OK.

"We raided the President's orchard!" I tell her, "Do you have any idea what the police would do with someone who did that in Washington DC?"

"Don't try that in Stockholm," is Ice's reply.

In Stockholm that spring, thousands of Swedish students tried to march to their parliament to protest educational "reforms." Police swinging nightsticks attacked the front ranks of the marchers as they crossed a bridge. Everyone retreated. A few students broke dozens of store and hotel windows on the way back to campus.

Ice

I tell Ice I marched in America's capital last fall with tens of thousands of other people opposed to the Vietnam War. First, we held a big anti-war rally at the Lincoln Memorial. Then we marched across the bridge to Virginia. Our not-so-secret plan was to surround the Pentagon with a mass of people and shut it down.

I was a parade marshal near the Potomac River. Row after row of people of every description marched past me: old and young, White Black Latino and Indian, adults and children, students dressed in black and waving red flags, union members with banners and executives wearing suits and ties.

When I saw smoke rising from the Pentagon I ran across that bridge. The smell was still strong when I got there. It was tear gas.

People told me the front ranks of the marchers rushed ahead, flattened a makeshift fence, and charged the Pentagon's front entrance. They got in and guards tossed them out. Then hundreds of soldiers marched out, shot off tear gas, and pushed people further back, threatening them with bayonets. The troops shielded the building from the thousands of arriving protestors.

We all stood around for a long time without doing anything. I knew who the leaders were and they were nowhere to be seen. People were asking, "What do we do next? What do we do next?"

At the Pentagon that day, flower power tried to convince soldiers to join us. (They did not.) Hippies chanted mantras to levitate the Pentagon. (It stayed put.) And hundreds of young men publicly burned their draft cards (me included.)

In Vietnam, it was another day men, women, and children died because of land mines, bombs dropped from airplanes, shells fired from artillery, and all the other acts of war.

I decided to follow the action and walk around the Pentagon. I was surprised; all the troops and protestors were in one small area. I talked with four Japanese tourists returning to their car in the crowded parking lot on the opposite side. They enjoyed their afternoon visit to the Pentagon. They entered without any problem, took the tour, even bought souvenirs in the Pentagon gift shop.

The next day the media did not cover the mainstream politicians, union leaders, and Vietnam veterans who gave speeches at the rally.

The media publicized attractive young people putting flowers into gun barrels, weird looking hippies chanting, and young men like me dressed in suits and ties burning our draft cards.

Our dismal failure to do what we threatened, surround the Pentagon and shut it down made the anti-war movement look weak.

People against the war realized we had to do something else. Some decided to fight the draft, others to win the next election.

I supported "The Resistance." They had an office where young men not wanting to be drafted could receive counseling. (My own date with the draft board comes after my graduation next May)

I also put on my suit and tie again, and worked for the presidential campaign of Senator Eugene McCarthy. On Pennsylvania's Primary Election Day, I was a poll worker and talked to voters all day long. Most had made up their minds years ago. Everyone was very nice to me but McCarthy lost locally and statewide to the pro-war candidate Hubert Humphrey.

In most state primaries, Americans stood behind the war effort even as President Johnson and his Secretary of Defense, Robert McNamara were privately having second thoughts about it.

Ice has no opinion for or against the Vietnam War. "It should not be the concern of neutral Sweden."

"What about people suffering? What about murder?"

We go back to stories about traveling.

Ice says, "Tell me about Berlin."

Traveling to Berlin was another time I did not hitchhike. I tell Ice flying is the only way to get into Berlin because police prevent hitchhiking near communist East Germany. Besides, the round-trip flight from Hanover to Berlin cost only $20 and I had the twenty dollars from my Uncle Joe, who was an American soldier in World War II. Using his gift to visit the two Berlins was very special.

In 1961, the communist East German government put up concrete walls, barbed wire, and gun towers to stop their citizens from fleeing from East Berlin to West Berlin. People were leaving because life in the East was intolerable or life in the West looked better. Now people are still trying to get over the wall even with the knowledge they might be shot and killed.

First, I tell Ice about West Berlin. Evidence of the city's shelling and capture by Russian troops is easy to see if one is looking for it. Bullets holes scar the exteriors of older buildings. Craters from artillery explosions still mar concrete retaining walls and bridge abutments. However, most of West Berlin has been rebuilt since the end of World War II.

In the center of the city is a large green park with a big lake. West Berliners relax there. The lake is big enough for ships to be on. The ships are restaurants where people also go to dance. As I sat in the park my first night it was soothing to hear an orchestra playing a waltz from across the water.

I walked on many boulevards lined with trees, benches, and wide sidewalks. The streets have first floor shops or restaurants with apartments above. Everywhere are sidewalk cafes.

The West Berliners love their city. At night, I saw thousands of people just out walking on the sidewalks, sitting on benches, or in the cafes. People were talking to one another and happy to talk with me. I never heard the attitude of people imprisoned behind guard towers and barbed wire.

Ice wants to visit Berlin.

East Berlin is an entirely different city. Evidence of the war was easier to spot with many bullet scarred walls and barren ground where buildings once stood. I found no beautiful shopping district.

I saw a very gray East Berlin. The one park I went into was devoid of people. There were very few young adults visible anywhere. The two restaurants I ate in were quiet. They reminded me of the place at the end of the road in Irun, Spain.

Ice was interested in the one time I did interact with some young East Germans. I was near Hitler's Bunker. All the signs were in German; how was I to know lying down on the grass was forbidden? I closed my eyes and rested in the bright sunshine. Then I opened my eyes and there were these two young soldiers with sub-machine guns standing over top of me.

Soldiers had pointed guns at me in Spain but this time it was different. I was not afraid. I sat up, stood up, and walked over to the sidewalk. Then the soldiers returned to their jeep. I even felt safe enough to walk back onto the grass and retrieve my map and sunglasses. The soldiers stared at me but they kept their weapons in their laps.

In most other cities I visited in Europe, I met someone who acted like an ambassador, had pride in their town, and showed it to me. But in East Berlin there was no one like that. How can people walking around looking at the ground see a young visitor's smile? The East Germans may have put up the walls but they were the ones who were imprisoned.

Our Chinese food is finished. Ice says she has to get up with the sun to go to work. We split the bill. Outside, we feel a chill in the air. Thick clouds hide the moon and stars. We catch a late bus back towards her house and the dirt road.

I do not expect her to get off the bus with me but she does. It becomes pitch black as the bus pulls away. As we walk to the cabins, she holds the flashlight and I put my arm around her waist. There is a strong wind blowing. It moves the trees and gives them voices. I like that sound.

I do not expect her to take me past the screen door to my cabin but she comes right in with me. She lights the candle and sits down on the hard wooden bunk across from mine.

I go sit down close to her but I don't touch her. She doesn't move away. I put my hand on her back. I turn and touch her leg, and thigh. She lets me, but doesn't touch me.

Then we lean together shoulder to shoulder.

I tell her I am very glad I came to see her in Sweden. We had a great hike in forest together. We shared something of ourselves with each other tonight.

This is a good moment.

The candlelight is flickering.

Every Swedish person I have met so far has been very direct so I look in Ice's eyes and tell her, "I would love to make love with you. And I know how we can both enjoy the end of the evening." I move to kiss her.

Ice turns, and I kiss her cheek, her neck. She whispers, "Maria wants you," and "Maria made me promise to get you to visit her in Stockholm."

I stop. Ice even says, "Maria told me she has something to give to you."

I do not want the evening to end this way. We talk. My expectations had been raised by the last twenty minutes and now my feelings are upside down.

We talk but I do not pout, whine, or guilt-trip Ice. That was me years ago when I was still a virgin.

166

I ask Ice, "Why not? I will be gone tomorrow and us making love will be our secret. Your parents will never know. No one ever needs to know."

Again my words surprise me. Again I tell myself to stop. I don't want to be the kind of guy who says whatever pops into his head.

Ice answers, "I want sex with a man I <u>can</u> see again. It is OK if people know; in Sweden, sex is not something bad which needs to be hidden."

I know I agree with her answer; years ago I stopped believing sex was a sin. It does not need to be a secret. I have tied my hands with my tongue by saying something I don't even believe in.

Ice knows how she feels. She is not dumb. Telling her she does not really feel how she feels would be stupid.

I lift my hand from Ice's thigh. I realize she stopped leaning against my shoulder minutes ago.

The candlelight is still flickering. I stand up and tell her my plane leaves from Paris soon. Hitchhiking to Stockholm is out of the question.

I tell Ice I want to walk her home to make sure she gets back safely. She stands up and laughs.

She says, "I walked you here because I wanted to make sure you were safe. People get so lost in this forest they die." She will be fine. She grew up here.

Ice touches my shoulder and I get very warm.

"You should visit my cousin," she says. "I am not kidding," she says. "You could get to Stockholm in less than one day. Marie's parents will let you stay at her house."

This beautiful young blond Swedish woman bends over near the candle and writes down directions to Marie's house.

Now I am touching her waist but she is moving quickly to leave. Ice kisses me lightly, shakes my hand, and is out the door.

Her last words are, "Joe, go visit Marie."

CHAPTER 8

DARKNESS FAILS ME

I take the candle with me to the outhouse. The wind blows it out and the world disappears in blackness. I cannot even see my hand in front of my face. But I have a lighter with me. I re-light the candle. I re-light it several times.

Inside my cabin again, I put the candle down on the small table. It flickers steadily. In other cabins, no lights are lit. I hear no voices. The trees are making a different sound now. I hear them creaking.

There is no solid door, no way to close the windows. Nothing keeps the winds out. And they are cold winds. Stronger and stronger they are blowing and louder. I can feel the temperature dropping. The candle goes out and I don't try to re-light it.

This sleeping bag is my friend now. I take back all those things I thought about it during the light of day. The hard wooden planks of the platform bed make a better bed than the earth, and a much better bed than the side of the road. This is a good bed.

I take off my clothes, get in and get warm. Should I risk going to Stockholm tomorrow? It is almost 350 km away. Can I see Marie and still make it to Paris in three days? Those cities are almost as far apart as New York and Miami. Hitchhiking works but requires patience. I want there to be a way.

Why did I come up to Sweden? Why didn't I go to Amsterdam like everyone else? Those answers come easy. I made the decision after my worst hitchhiking experience and a bad blind date.

I close my eyes. I think about death near the French-German border. It was on a very dark night when a German man who lived nearby put me out on the side of a highway. The man's explanation was how the intersection where he would turn was a terrible place to leave me. It was late and he was not taking me home with him or driving thirty minutes out of his way to drop me off at my destination, Strasbourg, France.

A damp, foggy forest surrounded me. The road had just one fast lane in each direction. I started to walk. I was alone for a while and everything was quiet.

Then a big tractor-trailer came barreling past me and the wind practically knocked me off my feet. It was frighteningly loud. If you stand two feet away from tractor-trailers traveling at highway speeds you might begin to understand my newfound fear.

There was no shoulder. I could only walk along the road's edge. The land next to me was dense with weeds as tall as I was. Black silhouettes of trees stood up beyond that. Everything was wet with dew and fog. I could not see well. Probably people couldn't see me until the last second. More cars and trucks shot by me so close they almost touched me.

I was the wet dog in the darkness you see lit with headlights along the highway. The speeding truck drivers felt pity but this dog was behind them in an instant. It would be dangerous to stop. No one was going to stop for me. I wouldn't stop for me.

I had to go back to where my last driver put me out, a paved area the length of two tractor-trailers. I am sure it was where truckers pull off the highway to get some rest. A curb separated it from tall weeds. There was no streetlight, no moonlight. I could barely make out the horizon and a single tall black tree a stone's throw away.

Although I could not see the ground beneath my feet, I walked into the weeds towards the tree hoping for a place to lie down and sleep. A few steps in and my shoes sunk into muck and slurped when I lifted them. I took one-step backwards and slipped, almost fell. I came close to panic. The tall weeds, the soft wet ground, the smell, I was in a swamp. My next step might put me in mud up to my knees, or waist. Could I retrace my steps back to the pavement? I wanted to sit down there. I had no other choice.

As a little kid, I camped out dozens of times in the backyard in a pup tent or under the stars. I joined a scout troop. We started camping in farmers' fields and nearby woods. The next year we were pitching tents in a forest and then really roughing it, hiking and sleeping along mountain trails. But I never faced anything like this. Up to that night, my biggest fears while camping were of snakes and rats.

Killing me, I worried about a tractor-trailer pulling in and killing me. I sat on the curb. Exhaustion set in. I toppled over. The earth was very wet. Weeds poked my skin.

I laid out my sleeping bag on the pavement, in a place where I would be lit up by a truck's headlights. I took a dirty white t-shirt and cut-off jeans out of my backpack. My heavy poncho went under and over the sleeping bag to keep it dry.

Like every night, I took off my pants and shirt and put them into my backpack. I got in the bag. On top of the poncho, I spread out the dirty clothes. I hoped it would look like a human being was sleeping on the pavement. It wasn't raining. I comforted myself with the fact there were no mosquitoes bothering me. And I forgot to worry about snakes and rats. Eventually, I fell sleep.

In the Berlin hostel, an American told me I had slept in the Black Forest. It was where many men died in battles during World War 2, World War 1, and during the Franco-Prussian war one-hundred years ago, and during the Napoleonic Wars sixty years before that. I had slept among the remains of countless missing soldiers, amid sites of great terror and terrible tragedy.

If he was right, their spirits did not bother me. Only my thoughts and the tractor-trailers going by shaking the earth did that. Compared to living everyday in the horror of warfare, one night sleeping on the road to Strasbourg was a piece of cake.

In the morning, a Frenchman picked me up. As he drove, I watched our road quickly become elevated above a swamp. We passed an intersection supported on piers and raised above water. I did not even see a sidewalk there. If that was where the German driver was going to turn, where he left me was a far better place.

The Frenchman and I crossed an unguarded French-German border and he dropped me off near the beautiful cathedral in Strasbourg. Maybe this city was a destination for tourists but I went for other reasons.

A couple who lived there gave me a ride the week before and said, "Stop by and see us." They seemed very sincere; they gave me their address and phone number. They even offered to put me up for the night and promised a blind date.

When I called, the wife sounded glad to hear from me. She gave me directions to their apartment in a high-rise building. The place was easy to find.

We talked. Her husband came home and was surprised to see me. I said one thing I needed before the date was a bath. They let me use their tub.

Later, the young women arrived. The four of us had dinner and conversation in the young couple's dining room. I thought we were having fun.

Then my date and I had a private moment together on the apartment building's veranda. In that moment, she said goodbye and took the elevator away from me.

My blind date had complained to the wife, who told her husband, who reported the complaints to me. She did not find me attractive at all. I was not ugly but she did not like my unshaven face. My hair needed to be cut. My clothes should be pressed. I should smell better.

I asked and the man said he didn't notice any BO. I asked and he said she knew her date was going to be an American hitchhiker. "What did she expect, perfume?"

"Perhaps."

The outright rejection burned. I consoled myself. "There are women who find me attractive. I'm definitely attracted to some women." And I thought, "Attractive-attracted goes double for the two Swedish girls." Strasbourg was where my travel turned north to Sweden.

Now I am in Sweden, in a cabin in the forest and have no idea what direction I should travel in tomorrow. Right now, I want to go to sleep. It does not matter if my eyes are open or shut. Either way everything is just as black. There is knocking at my door. A tapping. I call out. "Who's there?"

No answer. I use my lighter and see nothing outside the cabin; I can only see the inside. I don't hear the tapping again. It's nothing.

My thoughts, the hard planks of the bed, the strong wind, the noise of the trees, and now raindrops falling lightly on the leaves all keep me awake. I tell myself tomorrow is another day. I can sort everything out tomorrow.

Louder sounds come inside. Long ago, camping taught me to expect all kinds of noises at night. They can be spooky and scary threatening noises but I try to hear a concert instead. The bushes and trees sing; the screens whistle and the winds chant. I repeat to myself, "In the darkness I always sleep, so the darkness is my friend. In the darkness I always sleep, so the darkness is my friend. In the darkness I always sleep..."

I have been lying here for a long time thinking like that, keeping positive thoughts in my mind. Maybe I have been sleeping, dozing on and off.

Mother Nature has many ways to get your attention. This one cannot be ignored.

A hard loud brittle CRACK of thunder shocks me awake. Rain is coming down and the strong wind blows mist into my cabin, onto my face. A bright, white FLASH of lightning, for one second, lights up the entire camp and the blackness rushes back. But I saw somebody at my screen door, looking at me! Immediately, CRACK sharp thunder happens again; I jerk upright.

My face is getting wet; lighting strikes close by; it lights up everything. And a shadow of a man is at my door, looking in. The rain is all over him. Instantly everything returns to black. And thunder's loud CRACK happens again. I fear what the next light will tell me.

Now my lighter won't light and I hear and feel

the rain pouring down. I see nothing. One, two, three seconds go by.

Bright FLASH, lighting, he's not there. For that second the entire camp shows up outside, a cold blue color pierced by strange black shadows. And I jerk at the CRACK of ear-splitting thunder. I'm getting wet; rain's coming inside the cabin, windblown through the screens.

People in another cabin are yelling. Lightning flashes. My shadow man appears and disappears. I think he had on a hat, and a striped coat. Thunder explodes; lighting strikes again. He's not there. More thunder, more lighting, he's a different shape.

Again and again, a dozen times in a few minutes, lighting strikes nearby and thunder cracks horribly. A storm from the sea is breaking on my mountain. The man at my door is only a shadow but seeing him has shaken me to my core.

The rain, the wind, thunder and lighting have painfully scared me. I move my bedroll to the dry bunk along the back wall. Time passes. The strong winds calm down to wind; the intense rain weakens to just a shower and the thunder stops hurting my ears. My pulse still races. I am alone and must deal with life.

My lighter works. I see nothing has changed but the color of the floor, now all wet. I lie down and close my eyes.

Long minutes go by. The rain stops. The
thunder comes from far away. I open my eyes again.
Light from the moon and stars pours down on the
camp and surprises me with vision. The camp is a soft
blue, like an old platinum black and white
photograph. I am very awake and filled with thoughts.

In that shadow of a man at my screen door, I
saw an inmate at Dachau. When I visited the
concentration camp, I saw old photos of him and
many men like him. When I close my eyes tonight, I
can see them again.

They all wear those striped coats and flat hats.
They all have their arms at their sides, are hunched
over and horribly skinny. I see them lined up outside
their barracks, standing at attention. I see hundreds
of their bodies lying in big pits.

I went to Dachau to bear witness about a real
place I only could imagine before. I saw the real place:
the sleeping pens, medical experiment torture rooms,
the gas chamber, and the crematorium. It was what I
feared. The buildings still had a bad smell, especially
the crematorium. Other visitors were crying. My
stomach hurt. I tasted fear there. Man's inhumanity
overwhelmed me. I saw Dachau on the perfect day,
dark and overcast. It was August but so cold I put on
my jacket. Then, as we walked outside and along the
rusting, ugly, barbed wire fence it rained. I cried.

Now I hear the loud dripping of water, from the trees to the cabin's roof and I hear quiet people sounds of movements and pleasant whispers. It sounds like a man and woman are making love in the next cabin. Was I wrong to let go of Ice?

Everyone who enters our life comes with their own thoughts and feelings. We affect no one's life without consequence.

I have not embarrassed myself on this trip with behavior that would have me shudder with bad memories. I will spend no time on a chair in an emergency room or a jail cell, replaying moments of poor judgment I wish I could take back and do right next time. I am not justifying mistakes to myself while practicing lies to tell everyone else. I am free to travel anywhere without fear a big brother or father or the police are looking for me. I can sleep with a clear conscience.

But sleeping is hard. Remembering is easy. Some German soldiers guarding the concentration camps stayed at their posts until relieved by Allied soldiers who immediately shot them dead. Other guards were put in with prisoners who promptly scratched them to death.

Imagine the look on the faces of those German soldiers who only did what they were told, and never asked questions. Had they thought about what they were doing? Did they know turning the tables is considered fair play? At the time most victors thought the losers got what they deserved. "Following orders" was (is) no defense. Life is consequence.

I am tired, wet, and chilled. I am on a hard bed trying to think about Seaside Heights and the New Jersey shore, about lying in the warm sun on a sandy beach or floating up and down on the peaceful waves. Maybe hours go by. Maybe I have been sleeping.

The sun is strong and the air is warm when I open my eyes so I know I did sleep.

There is no one else in the camp. I find the cold showers. I suffer through one quickly with soap and shampoo. I shave off my scraggly beard. You know why.

I take the bus into Gothenburg, eat breakfast, walk to the highway, and hold up a sign saying, "Stockholm."

Soon, a driver stops for me. I show him my map and he points to the east side of Sweden. His destination is over two hundred km away and two-thirds the way to Marie. I will be there tonight. I get in.

My driver does not speak English but his car does cough a lot. It is not an old car but it is a sick one. It struggles up the big hills. Then it dies.

My first ride has gone just twenty or thirty minutes into the Swedish forest and we are both standing here with the hood raised and I have no clue what is wrong or what I should do.

The driver however, knows what to do. He says goodbye to me, crosses the road, and waves his arm up and down every time a car travels by in the direction of Gothenburg.

Soon he is gone and I am there with his dead car. I try his auto-stop hitchhiking style, waving my arm up and down, not holding my arm out and thumb up. I think about how I planned the next few days.

Today is Tuesday. If I make it to Stockholm tonight, I can stay there Wednesday and Thursday and take the Friday morning train to Paris. I will be in Paris in time to catch my 5 PM Saturday plane to the States.

I have about thirty dollars left. If it is not enough money for a train ticket, I will start hitchhiking south tomorrow. That should be enough time. No sweat. The Swedes are a generous and caring people.

I agree to the first ride taking me away from the dead car even though it is only going a short distance. Very few cars are on this road. I wait hours for my next ride. I put away the Stockholm sign because I am still in the forest and Stockholm is two hundred km away.

On my map on this road is a big dot. A real city

is thirty km away. I missed lunch completely and it is almost dinnertime. I need to eat and I do not want to sleep in the forest tonight.

My next ride takes me to the big dot, the city of Jonkoping. I get out of the car in the center of town and there are many restaurants. However, something is wrong. Everyone I see is much older than I am. People are all dressed up. The men have on suits and ties. I hope I am just in the rich section of town because every restaurant menu is expensive and I am very hungry.

"Excuse me, do you speak English? Where can I find a place to eat that isn't so expensive," I ask the only young person walking by, a teenage Swedish girl. She smiles. She speaks English.

She says there is only one restaurant in town where food is cheap. All the foreign workers eat there. She is on her way home now and will walk with me there.

I tell her she does not have to go out of her way but she wants to. She also wants to ask me questions. Where am I from? Where am I going? What am I doing here? I try to answer, not long answers.

This young woman has been born and raised in Jonkoping. She says that Jonkoping is a resort for wealthy, older Swedes. It is not a destination for young people and especially not for hitchhikers. The attractions here are the fine restaurants and hotels, and the big lake we can see as we walk. I only see the nearby shoreline, nothing of the other side. She tells me there are several big lakes around here. They are similar to America's Great Lakes.

I see plenty of tourists around but she says tourist season ended last weekend. All summer, Jonkoping was crowded with older Swedes. Now, places are closing for the season and laying off their workers.

She agrees there are few young people here. It has been her problem. She grew up here and has never had many friends her own age.

She invites me to visit her tomorrow at her job. She works in the only record store in town. She says, "If you don't come in, the entire day will be boring."

What a great invitation!

This teenager says to me, "The City Fathers do not want young people to visit Jonkoping without their parents so young people stay away. Nightclubs are not allowed here. There is no place to go to dance. There is only one cheap restaurant. They will not build any inexpensive hotels. There is no youth hostel."

This kid is very smart and sounds like the town rebel. However, something she said troubles me. "Where can I sleep?" I ask her.

She says she will show me later.

Later, we walk by a row of one-story cottages with covered porches. Their wooden siding needs to be repainted. They look poorly maintained. She says the places used to be foreign worker housing. They are empty now so I can sleep on any porch tonight. She has seen hitchhikers sleeping here before but I should ask the police first.

"Ask the police first?"

"Do it to avoid trouble," she says.

I am thinking, "Where would I find a policeman to ask? And what if he doesn't speak English?" I am worrying about this but hunger is what I feel more than anything else.

This is a town for rich older people; I don't like it already. It sounds like I have hitchhiked into Palm Springs, California or Palm Beach, Florida. I hope I can get a ride out tomorrow. There is no train. I do not like the looks of this place. I feel very uncomfortable here.

She leaves me at the entrance to the restaurant. I easily could have walked right by the place. There is no big sign out front. It is just a one story high, cinderblock building.

When I open the door, I smell cigarettes not food. I hear many loud voices. I see the place is crowded, has a cafeteria steam table, and cheap prices.

1968 and I'm Hitchhiking Through Europe

Inside the cinderblock box are white walls, aluminum furniture, and a dirty floor. Fluorescent light bulbs give everything a cold ugly color. I buy my dinner and walk towards a table with a man my age sitting at it. He looks like a fellow traveler; we both have backpacks and bedrolls. His hair is two inches longer than mine is, and he has a full beard. He does not look happy and does not look up at me.

"Hi, my name's Joe." I say to him as I sit down. This introduction works in any language. It also tells the person where I am from.

Seconds tick by without him responding. I start eating. Finally, "I'm Bent." He is an American too.

Next thing, he asks me for money.

I ask him "Why should I?"

He laughs. He says, "I knew you were going to say no."

I did not say "no." I keep this to myself.

Now he wants to be my friend.

Bent begins to tell me his story and he does not stop for a long time. I don't mind; I'm hungry and eating.

He is an army brat. He grew up at so many army bases he cannot keep count. He went to a dozen different schools and hated them all. He is only eighteen but everybody tells him he looks a lot older. He has to go back and finish his last year of high school but does not want to. His father is a U.S. Army officer in Germany.

Bent has escaped his Dad's control for the summer. The U.S. army may have alerted German authorities to catch him so he came up to Sweden and has been here a month. He has not talked to many Swedes and keeps to himself. He just hangs around and floats from place to place. He has been in Jonkoping several days. He finishes with, "I hate this town. I hate all the rich, old people."

Wow, it did not take me long to find a mirror. Bent has reflected my bad attitude back at me.

He says, "Bent is my real last name." He does not use his first name and I don't ask him.

He tells me, "I got money. I just want more," and "When I ask, people put money in my hand." He calls these people "marks" and he calls them "assholes."

I am glad I did not give him anything.

Another young American years younger than us and with darker skin hears us talking and comes over. He says he too is an army brat. He too is hitchhiking around Sweden. The two brats talk. I talk little; I eat and listen.

These guys are misfits. I tune out their conversation and think about what has happened to my plans to see Marie in Stockholm.

Tomorrow is Wednesday. Tomorrow I need to find out how much a train from Stockholm to Paris costs and get up to see Marie or I have to give up and begin hitchhiking south.

The talk turns to the best place to spend the night. Bent knows where. It is inside a foreign worker apartment building. It is empty. He slept there several nights already.

They could be a team planning to rob me. As we get up to leave, I am relieved to see they are both one foot shorter than I am. With that kind of stupid reasoning, I feel more secure.

The three of us walk to the shore of the lake and sit on a park bench. Bent complains about hitchhiking and people. The kid listens and complains too. I figure they really did meet tonight by accident.

We have no beer to drink, no pot to smoke, or other drugs to take but this does not stop people from becoming weird.

Bent stands up and acts out how he hates any man who wears a tie. He thrusts his arms up and down, and jumps around. He hates everybody in authority. They are all on a power trip, he says. They want to take over our lives, not just policemen or army officers like his dad, but doctors, teachers, social workers, psychologists, and bureaucrats. He says, "If I could, I would kill them all."

Bent just said he would kill one of the kindest men I met in Europe. He was the man whose offer of a ride was more of a surprise than the family stopping on the auto-strada or the monk on the motorcycle.

I saw this man at the border between democratic Austria and communist Czechoslovakia. I also saw tank traps, intermittent gun towers, armed guards, tall barbed wire fences stretching to the horizon, and signs warning about minefields. Straddling the road on the communist side was a whitewashed customs station. In a line were motorists sitting in their cars waiting for their turn to answer questions before driving across the border.

I walked across the border into my first communist country and up some steps into customs.

A uniformed civil servant shuffling papers looked at my passport, not me. He wanted to know where I was going.

"Prague, the capital," I said.

He warned me, with official seriousness about what would happen when I left the country: all visitors must prove they changed five American dollars per day into Czech currency at the official government exchange rate. So right there I changed a $10 travelers check and asked for a receipt.

This man was my idea of a real communist bureaucrat. During the two-minute interview he never smiled. He did not give me a hard time. He asked questions and then stamped my passport.

I figured it was over so I went outside, walked fifty feet away from the building, and began hitching again. I stuck out my thumb as each car cleared customs and pulled onto the road.

Surprise; the bureaucrat came outside, got into a small car, drove over, and stopped next to me. Was I in trouble? Had I broken the rules already? I had been in a communist country for only five minutes. No. Instead, he offered me a ride to the nearby town.

I accepted. Not only did he give me a ride, he took me home with him for lunch. I met his elderly mother. We all sat down together and ate meat and potatoes in a stew. We shared delicious bread. The summer weather was a topic of conversation. The "reforms" in the Czech government came up. He said, "What reforms? I don't see any reforms."

I told him and his mom how wonderful lunch was and how much their kitchen reminded me of my grandmother's kitchen. Both had similar wallpaper, old photos of family, and brown enameled metal kitchen tables. They both smelled of good cooking. The only thing missing here was an Icon of the Virgin Mary.

This communist bureaucrat wanted me to have a good visit to Czechoslovakia. He gave me lots of advice about traveling such as: "Carry some Czech money at all times. Stay overnight in our big cities, not some small town. Go to a university for housing, never drink beer in a park or sleep outdoors." He also told me never to get into trouble with the police.

Lunch ended. He needed to get back to work, and wished me a good journey. I said I hoped he would have an interesting afternoon and thanked him and his mother for the wonderful meal. He and I parted as friends.

He could have driven right by me as he went home for lunch, but he stopped. No one ever had to give me a ride in their car or set a place for me at their table but people did.

When I started my trip, I knew nice waitress service brings bigger tips and a good store clerk talks to customers and says, "thank you." I knew about "commercial friendliness."

Here was genuine friendliness from a communist bureaucrat who took me home and introduced me to his mother. The three of us shared the lunch she made for the two of them. We enjoyed conversation. He expressed concern for my safety and they bid me a fond farewell.

I can't tell this story to Bent and the kid. They would dismiss it and me too. Bent hates all bureaucrats already. He is angry. He and the kid don't talk about anything positive. They talk about getting even and putting something over on somebody. What they are really doing is creating something else to complain about. Their complaints sound like children whining.

Would they learn something if I told them about the very next man I met in Czechoslovakia? He was the man who cried.

After lunch with the bureaucrat and his mother, I started hitchhiking again. I did not wait long before a car stopped. The driver was a Czech. He was a good-looking man about forty years old, lean and muscular with sharply chiseled features. He had short blond hair and looked like Jeff Chandler, the movie star.

I showed him the road map of Czechoslovakia and he pointed at a town halfway to Prague. I was happy to get a long ride. We just drove along quietly for the first ten minutes or so and then, in English he tells me he was just released after serving twenty years as a prisoner.

I had no idea what to say next. We had a conversation with many long pauses.

"Why would anyone put you in jail for twenty years?" A stupid question to ask any ex-inmate you meet is "What did you do?" and I had just done that.

Two minutes go by in silence.

"I am very sorry you were in prison for such a long time. That is very hard."

Another long pause.

He answered, "I wasn't always in prison." The car was quiet.

Twenty years ago members of the Czech communist party, who only got one-third the vote took control of the police and the government bureaucracy. Soviet troops were not even in Czechoslovakia then. The communists did this openly, through manipulation, intimidation, and determination while most people ignored politics. After they took control of the government, they arrested protestors and members of the other political parties.

"Did you get arrested for opposing the communists?"

Two minutes later, "I was arrested for being young and stupid."

I was thinking he has an automobile in a country where most people do not have cars. He looks in excellent physical condition. His command of English shows he had a very good education. My observations only lead me to doubt the veracity of his story. In 1949, the victors released political prisoners, or so I read. Five years later, they rounded up opposition leaders and "weak" communist party members and executed them.

"Why did they keep you in jail for twenty years for being young and stupid?" I had to ask.

"I told you I wasn't always kept in jail. They kept me wherever they wanted to keep me." He opened up. This man had been a carpenter and in prison, he became a master cabinetmaker.

He said, "They kept me a prisoner to work on the homes of the new rulers of Czechoslovakia. I worked with other prisoner-carpenters." They worked freely at first because they got special privileges. Next, the threat of no privileges got them to work. A year spent back in a jail cell was also motivation. The return of privileges came next.

Why the authorities made him work like this for twenty years should not surprise anyone. They were the law. Absolute power corrupts absolutely. If you do not understand why he went along you should look into your own heart.

The former prisoner said he is old. He was almost crying. He told me, "I lost the years when men get married. I will never have a wife and family."

I told him he could still do that; he wasn't old.

He said his freedom was most important. His new boss lent him the car to go to his next job. He will be paid for his labor. He goes home at night to his own apartment. He is not angry. He is a free man. (But this is a communist country.)

I ask if he should escape to the West and to real freedom.

He says he does not want to be a foreigner in somebody else's country. He loves Czechoslovakia. And he knows what freedom is, and is not. He tells me he is educated and says, "The West has no monopoly on freedom."

He kept talking. He explained how he got his freedom. After twenty years as a prisoner, everything became black. "I cried." He told me. "I cried everyday." He could not work anymore. They let him go. He said his life lived in darkness is over.

Bent and the kid have nothing to say.

I tell them it's late. It might start to rain. It is time for Bent to show us the place he promised was a good place sleep.

Bent leads us though back streets and alleys to a row of three story apartment buildings. Bent tries the front door to one building; it is locked. He says something and then tries another door. It is locked too. Finally, he finds one unlocked. The kid and I both express discomfort with this but Bent lies to us and we go inside and upstairs.

I absolutely need a place to sleep. We spread our sleeping bags out on a rug on the third floor landing in front of doors to three apartments. "Is this the good place to sleep we were promised?" I ask.

"Shh" from Bent meets my disapproval. I wish I went to the porches instead but finding them now would be impossible.

It is dark. I am feeling exhausted, falling asleep. Then it happens. An apartment door opens up a couple of inches. A bright white shaft of light from falls onto Bent, the kid, and me sprawled out at the top of the steps.

The light burns my face. I see the shadow of a head. I clearly see an eye staring through the crack. Before I can say, "I'm sorry" the door closes. I say it anyway.

"Shut up" orders Bent.

"I think we're in trouble," I whisper back.

With the low, grumbling voice of an old man, Bent disputes this. "What are they going to do, climb over us to go get the police?"

The kid is not talking. A minute goes by. Bent whispers, "They're foreign workers. They're afraid to call the police."

"They might call. You don't know."

The last thing I hear is "They don't have phones. Shut up." We are all quiet.

The darkness has been violated. My sleep postponed. Soon, from the regular sound of their breathing I can tell Bent and the kid are sleeping deeply.

Darkness Fails Me

I close my eyes but still feel the bright light shining on our faces. I sleep but strong dreams wake me throughout the night. Before the morning light chases the darkness away, I am wide-awake. But I have not rested.

CHAPTER 9

NEVER SAY THINGS CAN'T GET WORSE

I am the first one awake. Quietly, I try to roll up my sleeping bag and leave but Bent and the kid wake up too. They follow me outside. We're in an early morning fog. It isn't really dawn yet. We talk in the street, away from the buildings, near the sidewalk and some tall trees. A streetlight is on.

Bent starts first. He is pleased with how well everything went last night. "We're a team," he says. He wants us to join up with him.

I tell him to forget it.

The kid is even more upset about sleeping on the landing than I am. He looks like he's going to cry. He whines about last night. He's dirty. He has never been so scared in his entire life. And he blames me!

I don't deserve the blame. Bent is the one who said he knew a good place to sleep. Bent is the one who said the apartments are empty.

I point my finger at Bent. "He's the great leader. We both followed him." I mimic Bent's voice: "Oh, I'm forgetting what building it was,'" Bent said that as he turned one locked doorknob after another. 'Oh, this is the empty building; I'm sure. I slept here last night."

Under his breath, the kid curses at me. Bent keeps his mouth shut and I have no energy to argue. Slowly, the kid walks away backwards. He tugs on his clothes, gives me the finger, and puts on his backpack.

I watch the kid storm off and I look at Bent who is not looking at anything. A quick shiver goes through me. Maybe Bent is looking for his first fix of the day.

Bent turns to me and says, "You owe me one."

Do I owe him something because he found me the bad place to sleep last night? I could have done a better job without him. And where was Bent a minute ago? How could he ignore what I just said?

Maybe it is just too early for sarcasm because neither of them got it.

In the hazy morning light, Bent looks like he is in his mid-twenties, not eighteen. The age difference, his dirty appearance, possible drug addiction, and our foggy street corner all give me the creeps. No one else is around.

I tell him I owe him nothing. I trusted him last night but after he said he knew a good place to sleep and then took us to the landing, I am not trusting him again.

Bent acts hurt. He gives no apology and makes no excuses. He says things like "Everything worked out fine. We could have slept in a place a lot worse. All's well that ends well."

My back hurts. I am dirty, exhausted, and feel sick at my stomach. I do not call that ending well. I tell Bent, "People in the apartment could have come out and taken your money while you were sleeping."

He drops his backpack and starts looking through it. I want nothing more to do with him. I say, "We shouldn't spend any more time together. Let's go our separate ways, act like we don't even know each other."

Bent stands up. He tells me I'm just scared. I would be lost without him. "We're a team," he says. "Let's go have breakfast together." And he is throwing his arms around as he did when he was talking last night.

I turn my back on Bent outside the apartment building and head in the direction I hope the foreign worker restaurant is. Maybe he follows at a distance. I'm not sure.

Eventually, I find the restaurant. I try the doors, but they're locked. I look inside. A man is busy setting up tables but the place is not yet open. I decide to walk around the block, check for a tail, and come back in five minutes.

Around the corner from the restaurant, I see a laundromat with its doors wide open. I duck inside. The place smells good. It is clean, warm, dry, and deserted. I'm going to hide in the bathroom for five minutes. I sponge bathe. My pants get wet and I take them off. From my backpack, I pull out clothes I never want to wear again and put them on.

I walk over to a washing machine and in goes everything else I own plus detergent. Swedish washing machines are not difficult to figure out. They work like machines back home.

I am so exhausted I forget about wanting to eat and leave town. I sit on a bench in the corner and lean against my bedroll. Next, I am using it as a pillow; I have not slept well in days; I am sound asleep before I even think about what a bad idea it is.

Next thing I know, an old woman wearing a babushka is poking me. She is waking me up. I am not alone anymore. Women and children fill the laundromat. Not one of them appears to be Swedish.

I look in my washer. Surprise, my clothes are gone! <u>It must have been Bent!</u>

I panic of at the thought of wearing what I have on all the way back home. What would people think if I show up at the Paris airport wearing only a very dirty, torn white T-shirt, filthy cut-off jeans, and sandals?

Quickly, I start opening all the other washers but the woman who woke me up pulls me over to a table where my clothes are in a neat pile. They are clean, dry, folded, and still warm.

She did my laundry and let me sleep. She does not speak English but she understands I am grateful when I give her a U.S. dollar. Then I go back into the bathroom and change into clean clothes.

As I walk out, all the customers ignore me. Moms are talking. Kids are running around and the woman who did my laundry is not there to thank again. No one looks up as I leave. I wonder what they think of this stranger sleeping (snoring?) in their laundromat.

I look at my watch. It is late. This morning did not go as planned. I wanted to be halfway to Stockholm by now. Breakfast at dawn was what I wanted.

Now I am eating a late breakfast-almost lunch at the foreign worker restaurant. At least Bent is not here. If he had been waiting here for me, he couldn't wait as long as I slept at the laundromat.

Anytime I'm hungry food is good, and 25 cents for breakfast makes it taste even better. I need a second cup of coffee and I need to decide what to do next. The time to make it to Stockholm and Marie is rapidly disappearing. Just 72 hours separates me here in Jonkoping from when I need to be in Paris.

Maybe the young girl in the record store can help me learn the price of the overnight train from Stockholm to Paris. Seeing her again is a good idea. Finding the only record store in town will be easy. I will just ask someone who looks like a local, "Excuse me. Do you speak English? Do you know where the record store is?"

It is a nice hike to the center of town. The first person I ask walks me the two blocks to the store's front door. My good luck, she is here and smiles as I enter. She is the only employee and has just a few customers. The shop is about the size of a big living room and I see four, glass enclosed cubicles in the back. Bins fill the floor area and records leaning up against records fill the bins.

We exchange "Good morning." I do not want to tell her anything about last night except the food was good at the foreign worker restaurant. I thank her for walking me to the place.

The cubicles? They are for listening to the record you're interested in so you can decide if you want to buy it or not.

"Why would a store unwrap a brand new record album and let customers listen before they buy?" I ask her.

"Why would anyone spend money on a new album they never heard before?" is her reply.

I tell her I like the Swedish record store system. She is surprised and says, "Can't Americans also listen to albums before they buy them?"

"No."

"What would you like to listen to?" she asks.

"Do you have any James Brown records?"

"Who is James Brown?"

"He is the Godfather of Soul. He mixes up rock and roll, gospel music, and a big band with grand showmanship. He gives an amazing performance. James Brown gets the entire audience on their feet, dancing. His show was so good, I saw it twice."

She's heard soul music on Armed Forces Radio and likes it. She wants to know more so I tell her about James Brown and seeing him perform at the Midnight Show at the Uptown Theater in North Philadelphia.

I start naming popular soul groups I saw perform at my university: The Four Tops, Gladys

Knight and the Pips, Smokey Robinson and the Miracles, and The Temptations. All have great soul albums out. She starts writing down names. I tell her about Detroit and Motown.

"Maybe I can order some of these albums for our store," she says. No one back home would ever take my advice about music but I share my favorites with her.

"Write down Otis Redding too. His music's great. It's a shame he died last year"

I ask if the store has any BB King or Olatunji, or the Butterfield Blues Band album, *East-West*. That last group is an inter-racial urban band led by a white guitarist, Mike Butterfield and Olatunji is a Nigerian.

You can hear the rhythms of Olatunji's Nigerian drums in soul music, new style blues, and even English rock and roll.

White American college students have adopted soul music as a way to show they are not racist. And the music is great for dancing.

She asks for names of other groups popular with American college students.

"Lots of people I know like Jefferson Airplane." I tell her about Grace Slick. The group lives in a commune in San Francisco and they share their lives with everyone around them. They are real, not phonies. People can even crash at their commune.

They make great music together. I try to sing their song *"Somebody to Love,"* from their album, *Surrealistic Pillow*. The lyrics start, "When the truth is found, to be lies..."

She thinks I'm funny. She says the only album here like what I'm taking about is Jimi Hendrix's *"Are You Experienced?"* I love Jimi Hendrix's music. His songs are popular with urban, white working class kids. He has crossed the racial divide in America as no other performer has. And I haven't heard him for two months.

My wonderful record store clerk wants to hear him too. She can unwrap his album because I am on the customer side of the counter. I do not have to buy it, someone else will.

We head to the listening cubical together. There is a cushioned bench inside with two sets of earphones. This could become intimate. She shows me how to operate the sound system.

But we are not alone. She has other customers so she stops, leaves, and waits on one of them. I end up going back to the counter to be with her.

I ask how much money a one-way train ticket from Stockholm to Paris costs.

She is not sure.

I need to know if it is more than twenty-five U.S. dollars.

"Probably not that much," is what she tells me.

But she can't make phone calls from work. More customers come in and she has to stay at the counter. I take the Hendrix album, go sit in the cubicle and SHOCK, I see Bent coming in.

He comes right into my cubicle and sits down on the cushioned bench up against my shoulder. I do not say hi to him; he doesn't say hi to me.

Bent just says, "I'm going to take some albums and run." He predicts the clerk will chase him outside. He tells me to wait one minute, then put some albums in my backpack and leave. He knows someone who will pay us good money for record albums.

"I'm not stealing records from the store."

Now Bent only wants me to distract the clerk while he takes the albums. He says I can't even get into any trouble. Yeah, right, a guy like him went to my high school and at least one of his followers is already in jail.

I tell Bent we will call the cops if he doesn't leave right now, empty-handed.

Bent gets up and leaves the cubical. For the second time today, someone hurls curses at me and gives me the finger. He yells some kind of vague threat too as he goes out the door. Good.

I walk over to my friend at the cash register. She is upset. She asks if I know him.

I tell her about meeting Bent at the foreign worker restaurant and how he came here to steal albums. "I said we would call the cops if he tried anything. You heard him cursing me."

"My boss threw him out yesterday." She suddenly does not like being in the store by herself. She asks me to stay. She trusts me.

"I will stay until your boss comes in."

I am feeling a heavy weight come off my shoulders; hitchhiking farther north would be insane. Even if I got to Stockholm, tomorrow I will have only forty-eight hours to make it to Paris. Seeing Marie again is impossible *this year*. Instead, I will start hitchhiking south at rush hour. And I'm telling myself it's a good thing to spend the afternoon here with her.

We go back to talking about music. She likes songs sung by the Supremes. I saw them in concert. She wants to know what they look like.

I tell her about the young women who are the Supremes. Two are very thin and one is plump. When I saw them, they had their hair piled high on their heads, like beehives and wore fancy gowns covered with gold sequins. They gave a fabulous performance from a small stage in our college gym. The Supremes grew up together in a Detroit housing project. Now I bet the group is making about one-hundred thousand dollars a year, as much as the president makes.

"Are they Negroes?" she wants to know. There is no way to tell over Armed Forces Radio.

"The Supremes are three gorgeous women who are Black and beautiful." I explain Europeans called their African slaves Negroes (a Spanish/Portuguese word.) Calling people by the name they have chosen for themselves shows respect.

She thinks integration is important for Americans to accomplish. She read about Martin Luther King in English class and was upset at his murder four months ago. The rioting, burning, and looting in over a hundred American cities afterwards did not seem like the non-violence he would have wanted.

I tell her Martin Luther King's influence had been declining when he was killed. He was a great leader of the civil rights movement and fought for economic justice as well as equal rights. He gave speeches against the Vietnam War at small churches <u>and</u> big demonstrations. However, his non-violence was not ending discrimination in housing, lending, or employment. Before, just him showing up at a meeting guaranteed a good turn-out and press coverage. Now, the Black Panthers are grabbing the headlines by doing things like bearing arms (carrying rifles) while protesting inside the California State Capital Building and promising justice "by any means necessary."

Some people used the death of Martin Luther King to "get the goods," others used it to get even, but most blacks and whites deplored the violence. Fires in the ghettos destroyed the buildings people shopped at and lived in. I tell her everyone who cared about justice in this world was enraged about his murder.

She also brings up Senator Robert Kennedy's murder in June on the night he won the California primary and possibly the Democratic Party nomination for President. "Will the United states have a civil war?" she asks.

Her questions re-awaken my political passions. Just a few months ago, I saw the Bobby Kennedy give a speech in the same gym where the Supremes performed. Students packed the place. He spoke to our idealism, hopes, and dreams for a better world. The Kennedy voice/delivery/charisma had the audience standing, applauding, screaming their support. But his answers to questions from students were vague. He shared no plans about how he would end the war.

I tell my friend I support a real plan to end the war: Stop dropping bombs. Declare a cease-fire. Withdraw all American troops. Take with us the Vietnamese whose lives would be forfeit because of their positions in the French colonial administration and/or in the Saigon regime.

My side has a better plan than drafting every Vietnamese man under 35 to fight for Vietnam's cruel dictatorship. (Those soldiers will not win the war for us.) We have a MUCH better idea than more Americans dying and more Vietnamese being killed in order to keep their country "free" (meaning anything but communist.) However, many people are calling my side unpatriotic. Their voices are louder and more threatening then before. I don't care; they are the ones who drew a line in the sand.

They are upset about people crossing the line to the anti-war side. As Americans learn the history of Vietnam, discover what we are really doing over there (Operation Phoenix), and see no light at the end of the tunnel, they are changing their minds.

Young people are changing their style of clothes and growing long hair. Mustaches and beards are coming back after an absence of over seventy years. People are wearing buttons and carrying signs saying, *THINK ABOUT THIS.* (Not "Hooray for our side.") A new culture is springing up, the counter-culture. Appearance and buttons are ways of proclaiming to the world which side of this divide you are on. I like it.

Some of us think constantly about the way things are and the way things should be. It motivates us to speak up and act.

Differences over the war are ending life-long friendships. Arguments are provoking fistfights. Fathers are yelling at their sons, "Don't come back home again!" High school teachers are seeing their most patriotic graduates come home in boxes. I am speaking emotionally now. "And for what!"

I go on talking with my friend at the record store about a younger generation rejecting the mistakes of the old, the rise of the New Left, Black Power, burning cities, big demonstrations and counter-demonstrations, political violence, and all the open racial prejudice. I try to answer all her questions.

Finally I tell her, "I don't know if another American civil war is coming but it feels to me my country is already fighting with itself."

My country's problems make her very glad she lives in Sweden and she tells me, "I love my country." Swedish armies used to take over other countries but stopped about 300 years ago. War squandered the nation's wealth and men. Even one of their kings, Charles XII, died in a battle. (Now that's an idea!)

My friend supports all the good things the Swedish government does for people. She wants to become a teacher. Next year she will be able to afford to go to college. Soon her parents can retire. They worked hard all their lives and she says, "Now they're planning to travel."

We quickly talk the afternoon by.

She asks me about other places I visited and when I mention Czechoslovakia, she wants to know what the "Velvet Revolution" is.

I tell her some Czechoslovakian communist leaders are supporting a new climate of tolerance in their country. The government is relaxing two decades of oppression and allowing people more freedom. I think what is happening in Czechoslovakia is being portrayed inaccurately in our news in the West.

I tell her, "I was there. I saw it." I felt the exciting air of new freedoms in Prague. On a city sidewalk, I saw a man giving a speech and dozens of people listening to him. I saw people putting up posters and other people handing out leaflets. Vendors were selling many different western newspapers on street corners. People were listening to radio broadcasts of western rock and roll music and real news, and private moneychangers were standing in front of banks. I tell her all this happened completely in the open while last year all this could have gotten a person arrested.

People were still subject to arrest. The man who drove me into Prague took me straight to the student hotel. He said after midnight police arrest people who could not prove they were staying at a real address. He said it would be dangerous to sleep in a park or wander around Prague. "Threat to the public order" was the term he used. And it was after midnight.

But at the student hotel, there was no vacancy. They just turned me away. I walked out the front door and sat on the steps. Where was I to go?

The desk clerk came outside and had me come back inside. He said he was worried about me. He also knew police were arresting hitchhikers for sleeping in parks.

This man was a medical student with a summer job as the receptionist on the overnight shift at the student house. He told me his roommate had gone home for the weekend; I could sleep in that empty bed.

I thanked him a lot. He may have saved me from a few days in jail.

I stayed in Prague three more nights. Every morning, the medical student woke me up when his shift ended and I went out to see the city. In the evening, I returned before dinner and he was already up. Each night, we went out together.

The first night we walked through a crowded park and took a trolley for a tour around the city. Public transportation was practically free, like two cents. We stopped off at a working man's bar and ate cheese and mustard mixed with beer and spread on dark bread (delicious). My med student friend told me his plans for a great future in a new Czechoslovakia. After we got back to the student house, I went to bed and he went to work.

The second night we went down into a basement jazz club, sat at a table, and ordered drinks. Soon the place was standing room only. Most of the men were dressed in black suits with white shirts and thin ties, and the women in fancy, tight dresses. It seemed everyone held a lit cigarette. Spotlights filled the air above our heads with transparent tubes of bright smoke.

Four musicians came in. I saw a clarinetist, a bass player, a saxophonist, and a drummer. They played a long, spirited set of "*New York*" style jazz numbers. (The score contained two or three different rhythms played simultaneously.) The group hit the high notes well. The whole scene should have been in a movie.

The third night, I do not want to tell my new Swedish friend about the third night. I should call Marie and tell her I am sorry, very sorry but I must start back to Paris or I will miss my plane home.

"I loved Prague." I tell my friend about several conversations I had with people in Prague who were very friendly. They spoke English well and followed the news from other countries. Communist Prague was not like the sad, dreary city I saw when I went to communist East Berlin, the capital of the "German Democratic Republic" (communist East Germany.)

I ask where a nearby pay phone is.

She wants to know about East Berlin.

I tell her I saw a slow city with more police and soldiers on the streets than ordinary citizens. It is still bothering me that no one in East Berlin talked to me for the entire day. They seemed so conquered by fear.

"There is no disturbance of the public order in East Berlin. You can get in trouble for just lying down on the grass in the park."

Prague was treading on the edges of public disorder. A couple I joined for lunch at a crowded cafeteria quietly told me there had been an upsurge of drug use and street crime. They complained about people with no visible means of support who hung out on the sidewalk all day. She said, "Some of our sidewalks are only one meter wide so people standing around force other people to walk in the street."

I could not get this couple to tell me if they supported the new freedoms. The older woman told her companion, "Maybe we shouldn't be talking like this." He was a man who was young enough to have been her son. Why did she warn him, and in English too? I think they did not know what to make of this American with all his questions.

My short lunchtime conversation with those two people made an indelible impression on me.

So did several Czech boys with long hair down past their shoulders. They were teenagers wearing no shirts and hanging on the main corner of Prague, Wenceslas Square. Naked skin is a vision magnet for me, especially when it is among a sea of clothed people. In three days, I walked past these half-naked longhairs a dozen times. Sometimes I heard them arguing with older men dressed in suits and ties.

My new friend's boss comes into the record store about four P.M. They talk. He thanks me and I start to leave. I stop and ask her to join me for dinner at the restaurant. She seems pleased at the invitation but tells me she has to go home for dinner.

"I will start hitchhiking south now," I tell her. "Now is better than later." We say our goodbyes. She thanks me for staying. I tell her I really enjoyed the company of someone who asked me so many questions and was interested in my answers. And that she is an interesting kid herself. Her future sounds very bright to me.

Walking to the southbound road, I see a food store. Picking up some basics - fruit, candy, bread, and soda, might be a lifesaver for my trip. It is a well-stocked place, but the prices are high. I spend the money.

The edge of town comes up abruptly, after the last house. I am at the start of the only highway to the south, where Jonkoping ends and the forest begins. A bench is waiting there for me but something is missing.

I am sitting, eating my apple, and staring at a black road with a yellow strip down the middle. The macadam splits a big field of tall weeds into two halves. About a football field away, the road tunnels into a thickness of tall, dark trees. There is no gas station here. There are no suburbs outside Jonkoping, no billboards, no shopping malls, and there are no cars.

I watch the sun lower itself to the horizon, and the weeds turn a golden yellow. The dense forest grows even darker and not one, single, car drives by. I do not even bother to walk to the edge of the road and start hitchhiking.

I will stay in Jonkoping one more night. It's dinnertime. Drivers will be heading south in the morning, I tell myself. Tonight I will sleep on the porches.

Eating the apple ends. I put away the other things for tomorrow's journey. The foreign worker restaurant will be the next place to go. But I am not hungry; I'm thinking about being in an airplane, flying over the Atlantic.

I walk the same route as I did yesterday with my teenage friend and pass by the lake and the row of empty houses with porches. This time I orient myself and make a mental map to use when I want to get back here and sleep.

I get to the restaurant. It is the same but I feel very different. There is something about being ready to leave and having to wait, which makes feelings change. I want to be alone; I eat quickly.

Now I go to the lake and walk through the park looking at flowerbeds and the manicured lawn, antique lampposts, black paved paths, and comfortable wooden benches. It is a beautiful night, still warm. There is a cool breeze. Many people are walking around. The men are wearing suits and ties, the women nice dresses.

I sit down on a bench facing the path, not the lake. Even if this is a resort for rich older people, I can still enjoy my last night in Sweden.

But fear replaced joy when I was watching the sunset and saw no cars on the road. I realize my feelings could spiral downward now.

It is as if my trip ends in Jonkoping. The future does not exist. I am scaring myself so I think about how good and full my life back home is. I am ready to get back to America and college. This will be my senior year, a very good year. I want to see my friends and our house. In September, our anti-war coalition will begin working off-campus and forming alliances with unions, and neighborhood groups. We have contacts with students in the high schools now. I am getting behind the effort to link the war with economic injustice, poverty, and racism. At 21, I have begun to understand the ways of the world and in whose interests *the System* works best.

It is too bad so many activists are embracing the old language of Karl Marx, resurrecting words like imperialism and ruling class. Why don't they just point to how our economic system controls nations around the world and our soldiers are dying to keep it that way? Why don't they just show examples of how large shareholders of giant corporations benefit from the best laws money can buy?

The old language is used not just because short words have impact on protest signs. I have witnessed the sorry sight of members of the American Communist Party, the Progressive Labor Party, and the Socialist Workers Party tirelessly recruiting inside anti-war groups. The old left is organized, loud, and often influential. The losers are independents, religious peace activists, and the New Left. The losers are people who hear "un-American" words like imperialism and ruling class and keep silent about Vietnam.

The real losers are Vietnamese. I am sure at least a hundred of them died today from our bombs and bullets. The anti-war movement is going to end up fighting itself and fade away. The Vietnamese will have to fight the war to the finish.

I feel so bad Senator Eugene McCarthy lost the presidential nomination, and Martin Luther King and Robert Kennedy were murdered. We have no leaders.

All these thoughts have my emotions spiraling downward. I start thinking about seeing my family again. But I'm not feeling homesick. And I don't miss my roommates, or my friends in the movement. I am frightened about something else. I will not get back. My confidence has disappeared. The next few days will happen and I will still be hitchhiking in a forest somewhere, or standing at a gas station desperately making phone calls. I will be broke. At this minute I am too far away with too little time left and don't have enough money in my pocket. Soon, I will suffer the consequences of all my bad choices.

I am self-absorbed with my worries. I am not looking around. I don't see him coming. He jumps onto my bench and right up against me. Bent is shoulder to shoulder with me, and he smells bad.

I look at him. Maybe he is waiting for my reaction but I am speechless. He says nothing. And I don't even make a face at him.

He leans forward and puts his elbows on his knees, his chin on his hands. He doesn't say anything. He doesn't try anything.

One minute goes by, maybe two. He is not going to force me off my bench. I have nothing to say to him and it sounds like he has nothing to say to me.

We sit there. More minutes go by. He doesn't get cozy. We say nothing. I want him to be gone. Will he start a fight with me? Probably not. Can I sit here until he leaves? I can. I have more patience than he does. There will be no harm if I just sit here quietly and wait him out.

I say to myself, things can't get worse than this.

Never say things can't get worse.

Bent bounces up. I hear him say something like, "I am doing this for you." He takes three steps and a split second later, he throws a roundhouse punch at an old gentleman walking on the path right in front of us. It connects with the man's face.

The man's glasses flying off is a picture frozen in my memory.

Instantly out of me, comes a screaming "STOP." I don't know where it came from. It wasn't into my mind and out of my mouth. It was quicker than that.

The man is staggering. The guy he's with tries

to keep him from falling. Everybody in the park is turning to look this way.

Bent's second strike isn't quick. It is an awkward punch and the other man blocks it with his body. Then Bent hits the first man again. Both men are bigger than Bent. They might in their sixties but in less than three seconds, they are fighting back. Bent does not stand a chance.

One man tackles Bent. He starts yelling, "Joe, help me!" and he yells and yells this again and again. The fight is happening about one car-length in front of me. I am sitting on this park bench and I am not moving one inch. I am frozen.

The men push Bent down to the sidewalk. He is struggling to get away. They punch him several times. He is still crying out for me to help him. He's cursing. One man puts his shoe on Bent's face. He's twisting Bent's arm. The other man is kneeling on Bent's ribs; I do not hear that ugly sound of bones breaking. All three men are struggling, looking at me. They all have fear in their eyes.

Bent goes limp. He stops moving and starts crying. He is lying there about two car lengths away and is still calling out for help from Joe.

Now he's squirming around and trying to get up. The two men are trying to hold him down. I am shaking as if I was in the fight myself.

I want to push myself to the end of the bench, away from the action. I can't. I want to get up and run. BAD IDEA! I won't. I don't get the chance to do anything.

A giant Swedish Policeman runs over. Not one minute has gone by since the fight began. As he goes by me, he levels his nightstick at my chest and says something very harsh to me, in Swedish. I need no translation. He just told me I am not going anywhere.

Bent receives a swinging nightstick to his head. He stops moving; he is not making any sound at all. For a moment, I close my eyes. It's quiet in the park, with dozens of people within fifty feet of us and I know everybody is looking this way.

After another minute, all those people return to whatever they were doing before the fight started. Walking, talking, standing up, sitting down, coming and going all start happening again but Bent, he's unconscious, the cops and the two men are talking and looking at me and they start laughing, laughing loudly.

They are laughing at me.

I cannot move. I try but I cannot move. I am scared beyond any fear I have ever felt before. Do you know who the Gestapo were? In your town, do the police act like the Gestapo with strangers, or towards minorities and the poor?

I become numb to my surroundings. I stop looking around. My vision tunnels onto the scene immediately in front of me. Then right down into my face comes the face of the Swedish teenager who works at the record store.

She is inches away from me. I hear her say something like "You are very lucky." I do not understand, and I cannot speak. She tells me the cop wants to arrest me and the two men are telling him I did nothing except yell "stop." She says "stop" is what they are laughing about, "stop!"

"Can't you hear them saying 'STOP'?" she is saying and she repeats this several times.

She translates more of what they are talking about. The cop still wants to put me into the police car. Her presence is making me feel better but she is telling me I am still in trouble.

She says, "I thought you were leaving town before sunset?"

It takes me a minute to find my voice. I tell her about the bench and empty road-leaving town. She goes over and says something to the policeman. She comes back and sits down right next to me on the bench. She says nothing. I thank her for trying to help me but I am really scared.

I ask her, "Can I walk you home? I will sleep in your garage or the barn. If we can leave together, I won't spend the night in jail. If I go to jail, I will miss my flight home."

Other police arrive. They are all talking among themselves. She knows one of the cops. She stands up, goes over, and talks to him. Nothing. She comes back and says nothing but she sits down next to me again.

We both watch as the police pull Bent's hands behind him and twist on handcuffs. They pull his torso off the ground and set him on his knees, then raise him up on his feet. He is not unconscious. He is standing but not walking. He is making no noise. He's not looking around. He is bleeding around his mouth. Blood stains his shirt. They drag him into the police car and lay him face down on the back seat. The car leaves.

The cop my teenage friend knows comes over and they talk. She tells me "He has offered to drive me home and you have to stay here until he comes back for you. Do not worry; you are not going to be arrested. He will drive you to the porches. I promised him you would leave town tomorrow morning."

"I promise."

The teenager stands up. I don't, but I do thank her. I tell her she is a true friend. Other people might have walked away from a foreigner they knew who was in trouble with the police. Some people might even ignore a neighbor's plight. Her actions show she is a fearless person with a good heart.

I tell her she will always have many friends. She understands. She smiles, says goodnight and goodbye. Then she leaves me.

I sit on the bench as everyone leaves. The two men walk away. The other police disappear. Slowly, the minutes pass by, then a half hour, then an hour. The park empties of people. Time travels past midnight. Out go the lights along the path.

I am sitting in a park in the dark, alone in a small town surrounded by a lake and a forest in a country where I don't speak the language. And in the black sky, I see millions of beautiful stars.

How long would you sit and wait for the police to return and take you away?

CHAPTER 10

THE LONG WAY BACK

I wake up. The morning dew has made everything around me wet. I'm dry. It is a good thing I slept on this porch.

Today is the first day of the end of my journey. I tell myself, "Tonight, I will be in Copenhagen, tomorrow Paris."

The early morning sun is a bright gold ball burning in a slice of sky above the horizon, and below thick clouds. I turn so its rays strike my back. Its warmth feels wonderful. Sunshine makes me stronger. Today is a good day and around the corner is a good breakfast.

Last night was no bad dream. It was much worse than any bad dream for Bent. He might be in a hospital now. A Swedish jail cell is where he will nurse his wounds. But if his father really is an officer in the U.S. army, the police might send Bent back to Germany today. Maybe Bent is a deserter and the father part a lie. Maybe he was lying, period.

I did not like him but I hung around with him anyway. Why did I make that mistake? Was it because he talked as if he knew something?

How close did I come to going to jail with him last night? "I came this close," I say out loud, while holding my thumb and forefinger apart one millimeter. I raise my hand to my eye and the space is still miniscule.

Now he has me talking to myself. I will stop thinking about him. For me, last night is over. I have no physical or emotional injury. Just the opposite, I have survived a hurricane, again.

"It's GREAT TO BE ALIVE!" I yell loudly to no one. No one lives here, I trust. My friend from the record store showing up and helping me, was that just a coincidence? My good fortune is almost enough to get me to believe in Guardian Angels.

This summer I have made my angel work very hard. It has performed perfectly; saved me from every bizarre danger I have fallen into, and directed me to wonderful encounters with other human beings. My Guardian Angel must have ten thousand years of experience. I hope it is enjoying the interesting work I challenge it with. Thank you Guardian Angel.

What a wonderful thought; I have an expert, first-class, master Guardian Angel.

I should not kid myself. I have no idea if there is anything invisible at work here. From what I know of history, for even the most fearless or fortunate of people, there often comes a day when angels fails to show up. The sad experiences of many previously lucky individuals fill our newspapers. I am not home yet.

I have no Guardian Angel. I have been lucky, and treating people as I want to be treated has always helped.

Why did the Swedish teenager come over to me in the midst of all the struggle and fear? I stayed with her when she was afraid of Bent and we formed a bond of friendship. She did what someone should do when a friend is in trouble.

Not every friend will do that. She will grow up to be a wonderful person.

I will not go and see her this morning. We have already said our goodbyes twice. I need to get an early start. I need breakfast.

For the fourth time in three days, I go to the foreign worker restaurant. The cashier recognizes me. I recognize several of the other men here. We nod, but

I sit alone. People can eat often in this one place. The food is good. The prices are low.

I am thinking, "Eat well, who knows when the next hot meal with happen."

I finish and walk through a quiet city. It is early, before the stores are open but some citizens of Jonkoping are out. I guess they are going to their jobs.

Blue skies and some large white clouds are overhead. It is getting warm and there is a mild breeze coming off the large lake. Today looks like it will be another beautiful day.

I am saved! The main highway to the south has cars on it, not many but enough. If I wait one hour or eight hours, I will get to Copenhagen by tomorrow morning. Then I will take the train to Paris and the flight home. I am saved!

Waiting an hour in the morning sunshine does not dampen my good spirits. I keep a sign raised saying "Malmo." It is three hours south and where I can catch the ferry.

Some people driving by smile and wave. They are probably going a short distance to some place in the forest. I do not want to go there.

A few trucks go by, then a bus. Buses, I could be taking a bus to Copenhagen! I only asked about taking a train out of Jonkoping, not the bus. Chalk that up as another one of my mistakes.

I will try hitchhiking here just one more hour and then I will...

Now is when a small car pulls over. It is another of those, "Too small to be sold in the U.S.A" type of cars. I run to it. The man inside does not speak English; he does not look well.

On my map, the driver points to his destination, a town on the coast road between Malmo and Gothenburg. I traveled on that same road three days ago. It is a couple hours away and it will be a very good place to hitchhike to Malmo from. I can even get a good lunch there.

The ride begins simply enough. We are quiet. He lights up a cigarette. We take the main road south into the dense, green, Swedish forest I spent so much time looking at from a distance.

As soon as he finishes his first cigarette he lights his second. After the second, he lights up a third. He is chain smoking.

I do not like looking at the driver because he looks sick. He is coughing while smoking and perspiring heavily. He keeps wiping sweat off his face with a dirty brown handkerchief. His black hair is dirty and matted down. The fingers of his right hand are stained brown by tobacco smoke. He is gripping the steering wheel very tightly and is holding his body very close to it.

We are not even trying to talk. He is staring at the road. I am looking at the cars and trees going by. Then he pulls over.

The man gets out, walks away from the car and pisses on a tree. He comes back, gets in and drives. I hoped he would smile at me but he is acting as if I am not here. Nothing unusual.

Actually, this is very unusual. Even drivers with whom I did not share a language always attempted communication-verbal or non-verbal. Maybe he is different because he is sick.

We are sharing a beautiful, sunny, warm morning. The light brown raincoat he is wearing is torn and stained. We are sitting close to one another in this very small car.

We go two more cigarettes further down the road. Now I need a cigarette and light a Marlboro from a nearly crushed pack I bought weeks ago. European Marlboros taste harsher than American Marlboros. Both sell in identical packaging and the American ones are twice the cost. This is a European Marlboro. Bad taste is one reason I have not been smoking them quickly. Watching my money go up in smoke is another.

We pass an intersection and other cars turn here towards the coast. Our road's surface gets worse and we start driving over rolling hills. The trees thin out. I am in the middle of the Swedish forest. There are almost no cars on this highway. He pulls over again.

My driver gets out, runs next to some trees and takes a leak. He turns and looks at me. I turn my head. He comes back to the car, gets in and drives. A smile would comfort me but he is not smiling. He just drives, sweats, coughs, and smokes. We go one more cigarette down the road. I see an occasional dirt road that immediately disappears into the woods. There are no other cars ahead or behind us.

I recognize a gut feeling I am having. It is a bad feeling. This driver is someone I would rather not be with. What should I do? My option is the side of the road and that is not a good option. Except now, he pulls over to the side of the road for a third time.

Again the man gets out, runs near some trees but this time he does not take a leak. He opens a magazine, and for a long minute, looks at pictures in it. We eye each other. He comes back to the car, gets in, and restarts the motor. He stares at his crotch. He looks at me.

He shifts his body close to mine. Down he looks at his hands. I look too. He makes a circle with his left thumb and four fingers, and he plunges his right forefinger up and down, up and down in the hole his left hand makes.

His intercoursing fists rise up from above his lap into my face. He is communicating clearly.

One second goes by. My vision freezes on his plunging, dirty, boney fingers and his big brown thumbnail. One more second; I see his face again. His open mouth shows plenty of brown and missing teeth. He has bad breath. A third second; B.O. oozes out from his open raincoat. His two hands pull apart.

"NO" jumps out of me, "nyet" (Russian), "nein" (German) and "nada (Spanish)." He sits back. I never learned "no" in Swedish! I say, "no, tax" thinking that would mean something. He smiles, leans towards me again. "No!" I am sharp and loud with that no.

The guy leans away, turns his body towards his door, but turns his head back at me. He's looking over his shoulder and hiding his hands.

Is he fumbling with belt, maybe his zipper? What is he going to do? Is he going to expose himself? This man is frail, sick. What is he thinking? Maybe he's getting something out of his pocket, or up off the floor.

I am thinking, "Remember the lesson of the moving car in Spain," simultaneously with opening my door. He will not be driving me fast, down some dirt road at knifepoint.

His body is turning towards me as I am twisting around and pushing myself out of the car with my feet. I am falling onto the earth. Standing up, I'm taller than the car. My stuff! I am bending down, looking at him looking at me. I'm pushing the front seat forward and pulling my backpack out onto the dirt.

His face looks puzzled. I am feeling weird. He says nothing, pops the clutch, and hits the accelerator. I spin away from his moving car.

About twenty meters away he stops, leans over, closes the door and steps on the gas. Good riddance.

He leaves me shaking, with eerie quiet everywhere. My shoulders are hurting from where I hit the ground. And he drove off with my sleeping bag!

My upset feelings have my thoughts racing. I replay the last few seconds with a fight scene at the end. The first to throw their weight behind a hard punch to the jaw wins the fight.

No, fights do not work out according to plans. The spilling of blood did not happen to him or me. No explanations are due the police or to a doctor sewing me up. Better he is gone than sitting unconscious in his car.

I am still shaking, realizing I am very angry. And totally alone. Alone in the forest and I want to get home.

He has left me near the top of a hill. To the north, I see a long, bright black road. It looks like a ribbon that rises and falls on a series of green rolling hills. I can see to the horizon. I stare into the distance. Not one car is approaching.

Should I start walking? I am so upset I'm not thinking straight. This is trouble. I had better start thinking straight. "People die in this forest." Ice said.

I am standing in a clearing. The bright sun is right here. Elsewhere the trees shade the edge of the road with darkness. If I can see way up the road, it means drivers can see me from far away. This is an easy place for cars to pull off the road. I will stand here.

I change into my nicest shirt, the blue oxford cloth I was saving to wear when I met up with my friends in Paris and on the plane home.

I see one car coming over the most distant hill. Up and down, I see it several times. It is a dark car, small; maybe a French Citroen like the one Barbara drove. It comes closer.

Long minutes pass by as I watch this car drive towards me. No other car is behind it. The driver can see me. I do not have a sign up. I do not have my thumb out. Auto-stop, I wave my entire arm up and down, palm out, fist open.

Now the last 50 meters, I can see him looking at me. I stand straight. I do not want to look scared, angry, desperate; I try smiling. He slows down. He

236

stops in the middle of the road. He does not open the door. He rolls down the window the width of a hand, and talks.

I respond to what he says with, "I'm sorry but I do not understand Swedish."

"I am speaking Danish," he says in English. "Why are you out in the middle of this forest hitchhiking?"

I was not ready to talk about it. But, as best I can, I tell him my last driver wanted sex with me and I jumped out of the car. I suddenly sound like a scared fool to myself. Why had I been so afraid?

The driver asks, "Did you hit him?"

I am more afraid now than ever. "No. He just drove away. And he took my sleeping bag with him."

I really need a ride.

"I really need a ride now. My plane leaves Paris the day after tomorrow and I am afraid I will be stuck here."

He leans completely over to the passenger seat and looks me up and down. He is a thin, good-looking man in his mid-twenties, well dressed, with a neatly trimmed beard. He is wearing wire-rimmed glasses. He pushes the door open.

"Thank you thank you thank you."

There is no more talk before we are driving over the hill. Ahead of us, next to the road, my sleeping bag! He stops. I am thinking, "Should I get out and pick it up? Will my ride drive off and leave me here?"

I don't care about the bag. It is so dirty it might be impossible to clean. But it confirms my story. After he suggests I get out and pick it up, I do.

My driver's only remark is the guy threw the evidence out the car. He does not ask a single question about the incident.

A graduate student in electrical engineering is what he is and being a teaching assistant and brand new father is what he does. I am happy to tell him what I do.

Our conversation is not about Jonkoping or Ice. I am not telling hitchhiking stories. We are talking about being college students. This man is a good man. My deep fears are being washed away by what is happening now.

Time goes by. I learn he teaches at the university in Copenhagen. It is the biggest one in Denmark. I tell him I go to the University of Pennsylvania and it has 15,000 students.

American college protests come up. Talking is making me feel better so I start telling him about some of the things we did at my university.

A dozen of us staged a "sit-in" at the entrance to a college laboratory where germ warfare research was happening on campus. This got us some verbal abuse and good coverage in the university newspaper. Most students thought anywhere nearby was the wrong place for germ warfare research.

About twenty of us picketed the ROTC (Reserve Officer Training Corps.) I carried a sign saying, "The poor get drafted and the rich exempted." We passed out literature but most people walking by did not seem interested.

At a local church, a small group of students and professors held a "teach-in" every weekend; I went. Over time, hundreds of people attended and learned about the history of Vietnam.

American intelligence agents in Vietnam during World War 2 were angry at the French colonial government for collaborating with the Japanese. They knew the Vietnamese liberation army aided the U.S. during the war. The time for French colonialism was over; America should support the brand new government of a united independent Vietnam.

The agents asked Washington DC for advice. During the war, President Roosevelt had been sympathetic. After the war ended, the leaders of the new Vietnamese government appealed directly to President Truman for recognition. We know the U.S. supported the French who ousted the Nationalist government of Vietnam and started a war to keep their colony. {Pentagon Papers}

Fighting continued until 1954 when the French were defeated. They signed a peace treaty temporarily dividing the country into North and South until elections in 1956 would reunify the two zones. The elections did not happen because South Vietnam's Catholic dictator Diem knew he would lose the popular vote to the nationalist-communist leader of the North, Ho Chi Minh.

In 1956, the war for an independent, unified Vietnam started again. The North Vietnamese supported the new liberation army, the Viet Cong. The U.S. supported Diem. First, we gave him millions of tax dollars. Next, we sent advisors. Soon after that, our fighting men arrived.

It did not help America's side when Diem replaced every elected mayor in South Vietnam with someone appointed by him or began restricting Buddhist religious practices. (Vietnam is a majority Buddhist country.) Then Buddhist monks began setting themselves on fire in the streets of Saigon to protest religious persecution. Every year more recruits joined the Viet Cong.

My Danish friend says, "Colonialism is a sad chapter in the history of the world. " He tells me he and his friends used to think the U.S. was going to win the American War in Vietnam but he changed his mind this year.

Most Americans also believed frequent U.S. government reports about the enemy being severely weakened by our bombing and assaults.

However, on Tet (Vietnamese New Year's Day) January 30, 1968 the North Vietnamese Army and Viet Cong launched a major offensive. It surprised everyone. Coordinated, massive attacks occurred all over South Vietnam. Communists took over many large cities and executed collaborators with the Americans.

The American and South Vietnamese armies fought back. After one week, we declared the Tet offensive a big failure but the fighting continued. The next month the enemy was defeated but the fighting continued. By May, reports said we had won completely but the fighting was going on inside the South Vietnamese capital. {Today, some people still believe Tet was a big defeat for the NVA and the VC.}

Tet was the turning point. Americans en masse began to realize our government was lying and at a great cost to America.

Driving down the highway, my Danish driver and I have a lot of time together. Since he seems to be listening, I continue talking. I have other good stories, even surprising ones about what happened to people in the movement to end the war.

After Tet, I went to a campus rally where

people gave speeches against the American strategy of dropping napalm to clear Vietnamese towns. We gave speeches. A few of our fellow students came and threw coins at us; they spat upon some us.

Later that day, demonstrators walked in a circle carrying signs. That is when more counter-protestors came. They tried to bully us. They grabbed signs and pushed people around. Then they left.

These acts affected a few demonstrators so much they never went to another protest again. However, the next day we held an anti-war-free speech demonstration and hundreds came. It was the biggest campus protest we ever had so far.

I told him about the Philadelphia police arresting the leaders of a New Left group who lived together in a commune. Police and press entered their house, went right to their refrigerator and found dynamite behind it. I knew two of the young men arrested. They were "peaceniks." I smelled a rat; I thought police planted the evidence. Several carloads of us drove to police headquarters and set up picket lines.

The newspapers convicted the young men with front-page stories about police catching students with explosives. They smeared the anti-war movement as a bunch of terrorists. However, the prosecutor never filed any charges. Police just let the guys go. I never saw any of them at another protest but other students stepped up and organized new demonstrations.

When President Johnson announced he would not seek a second full term as President, happy students spontaneously gathered at the center of campus to celebrate. We felt powerful. A hundred of us marched three miles to Independence Hall.

I fully expected the police to block our route but they did not. Maybe they were happy about Johnson's speech too. There are actually very few people who really like the war.

At another demonstration, our group sang and yelled to disrupt job interviews when recruiters from Dow Chemical (the maker of napalm) came to campus. City police marched into the college building and announced they would arrest protestors who would not leave. A few people stayed and were arrested. I left and still feel bad.

Before, I never wanted to be arrested. Now I don't know anymore. I am beginning to see everything as good or bad, right or wrong. Life has fewer shades of gray; everything is becoming clearly black and white. I am becoming radicalized by the war and what I see around me.

The Dane says, "I was never in a student demonstration. I don't want to protest anything." He tells me Danish students support their government.

Denmark has none of the turmoil experienced by France, Italy, Germany, or Czechoslovakia.

I tell him I visited all those countries.

He asks, "Were the Czechs having an anti-communist revolution?"

"No," I tell him. Some communist party leaders want to allow more freedom.

Some hard line communist party leaders and "super patriotic" Americans want to take freedoms away. These fascists do not have the upper hand in either country but I know there are many Americans ready to stop people from demonstrating against the war.

"Have you heard the news lately?" he asks.

"No."

I am afraid he will tell me "Anti-war protestors were shot and killed in the U.S. last week!" But it is nothing like that.

He says, "The Polish army crossed into Czechoslovakia. All news from Prague has been cut off."

That shocked me. I want to hear more.

With a quiet voice, almost inaudible above the wind noise, I hear him say, "The border was crossed peacefully. There was no opposition at all from the Czechoslovakian army".

He talked so softly it was as if he were passing

on a secret. He adds how there is no news coming from inside Czechoslovakia.

I am just guessing but if there is no fighting maybe it's not an invasion. Maybe the Polish troops went there to protect the social order. Troops from the Soviet Union would go in and overthrow the reformers. Maybe the Polish troops are helping the Czechs keep their new freedoms. I am just wishing.

I tell him about my guessing and why I am wishing for the best, but fear for the Czechoslovakian people rises up and joins us.

What will happen to all those freedom-loving people? I know we all love our freedom. Sometimes being in charge is the most freedom. Teachers rule over students, bosses over workers, police and bureaucrats over people like you and me. But in a free country, the person in charge is supposed to obey the rules too.

If you were above the law, would you call in the army to stay in power? Would you butcher your own people? History answers that question with a "yes." And it gives the people's response: "Off with their heads!"

We are quiet. He may not have liked the way I talked.

Finally, it is lunchtime. A nice restaurant is where we stop. He has driven almost to Malmo. Even better, he says we are going all the way to Copenhagen together.

Over lunch, we talk about weather-type topics. Then he asks, "When did you start hitchhiking?"

"When I was 15 years old," I tell him. Everyday I walked a mile and a half down one long road to get to school. The hike took me almost a half hour each way. It was winter. It was cold and my feet began to ache miserably. "Growing pains," my parents said.

I do not know where I got the idea but one morning when I was late to school, I just put out my thumb and hitchhiked.

He wants to know if I ever got any rides.

I got rides. I got lectures. Six rides happened before someone took my name and called my father.

"What did your father do?" he asks.

My father asked for an explanation. I reminded dad how he and mom raised us to believe 99.9% of all people want to be good people. I asked my father, "Who would hurt me?" { Of course, 1968 is before TV and the movies overwhelmed us with fear of crime and suspicion of all strangers, even though most victims and their assailants are not strangers to one another.}

The way my parents raised us gave all their kids a wonderful, positive confidence when we dealt with people.

"What did your father do?" he asks again.

He did not demand I stop. Actually, my Dad told me he hitchhiked in the 1930's. He warned me not to go further than school with anyone, and made me promise to tell him about anyone who picked me up regularly. I don't know if he ever told my mother.

"And?"

So I hitchhiked a few more times until the weather got better. My father bought me a new pair of shoes and my feet stopped hurting. The next year I started high school. A yellow school bus picked me up on the corner near my house and drove me there.

I realize this man is asking only short questions and I am doing all the talking. Is that good or bad?

He surprises me. He asks if I would like to come home with him to meet his wife and have dinner with them.

"I live in a humble apartment," he says. "It's crowded with the baby."

I tell him it is a wonderful invitation; he has given me several reasons to smile today.

But first, he has to call his wife to see if a guest for dinner is OK. I understand. He calls. It is fine with her. I feel great.

We get to Malmo and wait at the terminal. This part takes forever. Then we take a ship across the water to Copenhagen. Our ferry is different from the boat I took four days ago. It is capable of carrying many cars and trucks. My friend and I wander around together.

We leave the sunshine in Sweden. Cool and cloudy weather greets us in Copenhagen. But this city looks better when you feel good, and when someone you like drives you around.

To get to his house we drive over many streets. Stores, restaurants and offices, houses and apartments, all exist on the same block. The old ·and new buildings give a nice style to the wide avenues. There are few cars. Many people are walking on the sidewalks. I see no litter anywhere. I have to remark about how different this is than in American cities I have visited..

My driver loves his hometown, and Denmark. He talks about how every worker earns a decent wage, even men who pick up the trash. And the waiters and waitresses do not need to be tipped. It was not until college that he even knew what a tip was.

We arrive at his place. We walk up the stairs to the second floor. The apartment is magnificent; his wife is very happy to see him. I introduce myself. She gives me a chair to sit down in while they go unpack in the bedroom.

The place has two bedrooms, a kitchen, a separate dining room, and a large living room with a bay window that overlooks the avenue. Nice rugs and furniture are everywhere. This is no humble abode.

I am sitting at their dining room table next to the baby's high chair, looking at an oak china cabinet containing a nice record collection, a stereo amplifier, and a turntable (not old "High Fidelity" equipment.) They return.

She is bringing in their child. He is big already, over one year old and he is looking at me with giant eyes. "Are you hungry?" she says to him. What a beautiful kid. They tell me about how they are exposing him to English by speaking English. He will grow up knowing two languages.

Dinner for all of us goes on the table. Conversation begins with my Danish friend's trip. He gave a lecture in Stockholm. His speeches, and our conversation, are in English. He says, "English is on its way to being the language of the world." The world needs a universal language.

I ask them about Copenhagen. They ask me about my city.

I tell them I live in a great city. It has a real downtown with huge department stores and movie theaters that look like palaces inside. Subways, trains, trolleys, and buses can bring you to center city from any neighborhood or suburb. Next to the downtown is the largest city park in the world. You can wander around on remote trails as if you are in some kind of wilderness. I have found old ruins and big mansions in the park. A great art museum is there too. I add, "And I know a lot of good people who live in Philadelphia."

Now he asks me to tell his wife about what happened right before he picked me up.

I did not expect this and feel uncomfortable. I give her the short version. The driver pulled over and made a pass at me. I got afraid about where he would drive next so I got out of the car in the middle of the forest; almost lost my sleeping bag. "Did I make a mistake?"

"No," they say in unison. Hitchhikers get trouble from bad people, lots of trouble.

I tell her about being happy with the way things worked out. Her husband was great because he stopped and took me out of the forest. No other cars drove by while I waited. I say, "I could still be waiting there right now." I feel a shiver. What I just said was true.

He says I looked strange standing on that road and he was not sure if he should stop.

"Your husband asked me questions before he would open the door for me," I say to reassure her. I change the subject and tell them what a wonderful apartment they have.

He says Americans all live much better.

I want to tell him about where I grew up. About all the poor families living in the neighborhood next to ours and about all those tiny student apartments in run-down old rowhouses near my college campus.

So I tell him the truth; not all Americans live better than he does. This includes American college students.

He says, "Europeans think only a few Americans are poor."

"The U.S. government says over 10% of all Americans live below the poverty line. That is not a few. It's five million families, twenty million people."

My friend says he does not know about statistics. "What kind of student housing do you live in?" he asks.

I tell him about the big old Victorian mansion I live in with a great bunch of other men and women. Our place is on a tree-lined urban street on the edge of the University of Pennsylvania in West Philadelphia. The ceiling in the mirrored living room is twelve feet high. We enjoy fires in the marble fireplace on the second floor. The yard has rose gardens in the front and back. We have the entire house. We rent it for cheap. It's a fabulous place.

"See," he says.

"See what?" I think. I want to tell him this was

not about me but about him thinking all Americans live better than he does.

However, I am not telling him anything else. I don't want to argue. My bad minutes at the Swedish party make me shiver and stop. Besides, the university is going to tear down all the great old houses on our block one year from now and replace them with high-rise student dormitories. How would I explain that?

But he goes on. "If we lived in America, our son would grow up in a suburban house with grass all around."

"So what!" I'm thinking. I grew up in the suburbs and it did not make me a better person than students I knew who grew up in the city, but I do not challenge him on that statement either.

It turns out he thinks most Americans live in the suburbs but more live in cities and rural areas.

I try to give a compliment. "Your situation here is very good." He lives in a big apartment. It is beautifully furnished. We passed by a children's playground when we walked from where he parked his car to here. There is a green city park nearby and somebody else cuts the grass. "You told me you loved Copenhagen."

"See" his wife says. "This is what I have been telling you. What we have is very nice." She talks about the little park and being close to other young mothers here. They have good neighbors.

He wants something better.

I am determined to say nothing but say this: "Good neighbors are the best. City or suburbs, if you have bad neighbors where you live is not so nice."

They talk right over me. I think they have had this conversation before.

"I want to stay here," she says. They can afford the rent and will save money. When he graduates and gets a real job, everything will be easier. Even now, they have money to take vacations. In the future, they will be able to afford a small cottage in the woods.

He wants to live in his own house, not visit it on weekends.

I say nothing else. After going back and forth over this topic some more with his wife, my Danish friend gives up and finally stays quiet. She gets the last word on the subject and I hope everyone is OK with that. I know this conversation will go on later and for a long time.

After dinner, he offers to drive me to a youth hostel. He knows where the best one is.

I tell him he has been too kind already, "Just tell me what buses to take."

He says buses do not come frequently at night and he <u>wants</u> to drive me to the hostel.

His wife encourages me to accept his offer. She asks her husband which hostel he will take me to.

"The best one," he says again.

"Will there be room for me at the hostel?" I ask. I say thank you. We leave. And arrive. There is room. I fall asleep easily.

And I am looking forward to tomorrow.

CHAPTER 11

SKIN

At the hostel, all men sleep in a gymnasium size room on the ground floor. I am the first one up. It's early, still dark, and I wake up thinking about <u>The Invasion.</u>

In the dark room, I quietly pull on my pants. I find the showers locked, as is the breakfast room. But I am wide-awake. I find the person who works the hostel's reception desk. He looks like he's been up all night. Maybe he has. I probably look worse. I haven't even washed yet and I woke up with high anxiety.

Prague has been occupied. He tells me the army of every Eastern European communist country has invaded Czechoslovakia. He is worried. Less than a hundred kilometers separates Denmark from communist East Germany so the invader is on his doorstep. Everyone is watching the news but no one knows the truth about what is happening.

"Where can I find the Herald Tribune?" I ask. I want to read this English language newspaper, printed and distributed across Europe everyday. I might not find the truth in it but several times during my trip I found comfort on its pages.

To buy it he is sending me out into the city. I finish dressing and start walking. The sky is lighter. There is a cool breeze blowing. I'm thinking about how this might become a beautiful day for us here in Copenhagen, not Prague.

The night clerk told me about a kiosk open 24 hours selling all the daily papers. It is a kilometer away. The long walk is on quiet streets. Workers are readying cafes and restaurants for their morning customers. I see men carrying tables out to the sidewalk and truck drivers delivering food.

With some difficulty I find the kiosk. On the front page of every single newspaper are photographs of civilians climbing on tanks. And the tanks are in Wenceslas Square - I was just there!

I look up from all the pictures and look around. Few people are about. The sun is down at the end of a wide boulevard and has just risen above the horizon. Its low angle sends bright yellow light raking across the fronts of large old townhouses. Their different colors and features, their various sizes, together make a visual rhythm I can hum. One large bus rolls by, then another. The street is clean. The morning air is very fresh. Another city that has been a delight to experience like this is Prague.

I do not see photos of fighting, or dead bodies on the street, or holes blasted in buildings. What is going on? The newspapers are in many different languages but they all have the same pictures.

I buy the Herald Tribune. My heart sinks. This is an invasion by armies with hundreds of tanks and thousands of soldiers. Some of the forces are from the Soviet Union. The article says Czechs are fighting back and being killed.

I remember the man who cried. He is a good man. What would he do if those corrupt rulers wanted his services again? Czechoslovakia's brief affair with liberty and justice is over. I get sadder. My eyes swell up. My throat gets dry. I am crying.

I fold up the paper. I will finish reading it back at the hostel where I can share it with other people. It is a long walk back.

A small park sits in front of the hostel and a park bench in the sun beckons me over. I will absorb the bad news by myself for a while. I read the headlines: "communist armies occupy all of

Czechoslovakia," "Austrian border sees hundreds crossing to freedom," and "Many students arrested."

I remember my medical student friend. He shared his plans with me for a great life in a new Czechoslovakia. I know he is devastated. I hope he is alive. Tears run down my cheeks again. I cannot control it.

I look up from the paper and look around. A dozen other men are in the park. Five naked young women are clearly visible on the second floor of the hostel. They are standing, each one drying herself with a towel, totally unaware the sunshine makes the entire width of the floor to ceiling smoked glass window transparent. I have never seen anything like this in all my life. I have to look.

I stare at the women through my tears. Two of them standing in the back are disappearing from view as they move away from the window. The others are still enjoying being in the sunshine. They are rubbing their towels over their bodies. The sunshine, I know, is warm.

I look down at the newspaper. It is wet with my tears. Inside, there are more pictures of citizens of Prague arguing with Russian soldiers and of families with little children fleeing over the border to Austria.

I look up. Another woman has joined the group. She has just left the showers, completely naked like the others. I see each one has a unique body, some thin, some heavy, tall, short, long legs or longer torsos. Each is endowed with breasts that fit. Now some aren't facing me. Not one is seeing me. All this beauty makes me smile.

I look at several articles about the invasion. I scan them for people's names or street names or just facts. There are no names or facts. How much of this reporting is just speculation based on rumor?

I look at the window. One woman is there, less than 15 meters from my park bench and just above the doorway entrance to the hostel. Stretch out your right arm in front of you; expand the space between your thumb and forefinger to the maximum. That is how tall she looks from where I sit. We are close, very close. She dries herself. She turns. I see all her bare skin.

I look around. Another man in the park casually looks up at the window and looks down to his papers, turns and talks to his companion. What are they talking about? The invasion?

A young woman is drying herself like you and I after our showers, dry ourselves. I can tell she likes being in the sunshine for a half a minute. Then she is gone. The window is empty. I should be serious. I was crying and smiling, and reading about the invasion of a country whose people I care about, and now I am looking at another women standing in the sunshine naked, rubbing her wet skin with a towel.

I look at the men sitting on park benches on the other side of the path. They are facing me. When they look up, they see the trees behind me. What would I have missed seeing if I sat on a bench with my back to the window? How would I be feeling? What should I be seeing; how should I be feeling?

It is bad, very bad somewhere but not here. I know I will go back inside and eat breakfast in peace. What can I do to help the Czech people?

My thinking challenges me, "You should go back to Prague and, and what-throw stones at Soviet tanks?"

America is not going to help the Czechoslovakian people. The U.S. government does not want "Socialism with a human face" to be a success. The rich old white men who run my country live very well without socialism.

I have spied on private moments in the sun. I look up. Now a woman is there. The sequence is very predictable. I do not have to see it again to enjoy it; the beauty is in my mind. Perhaps, like in some Greek fable if people catch me gazing at the girls I will become an ass to everyone. (In the fable, the peeping Tom's head changes into a donkey's head.)

Now is the time to go back into the hostel and

eat breakfast. I need to talk to someone. I hate the invasion but am powerless do anything about it. I would love a shower and anyone can watch me. But being stared at is something different. My thinking is confused. I get up and go inside.

Food first. Only a "continental" breakfast is available. The selection is tea, coffee, fruit, rolls, and Danishes (of course). I take plenty.

A crowd packs the benches around every table in the breakfast room. I am looking for a seat and thinking, "These must be the women I saw upstairs."

I do not recognize faces. How would I remember faces? And I thought all of them had beautiful tan skin and brown hair. That must have been the smoked glass window.

Half of the women around the tables are blondes. All have very white skin. Everyone is talking to one another in their own languages. I understand nothing.

Someone is getting up and I will squeeze into their place on the bench. On either side, people have their backs turned. Across the table, several very young women are eating and laughing and talking in Danish, Swedish, or Norwegian. Their side of the table seems like it is far, far away. I feel weird.

No one makes room for me on the bench. It is not easy to squeeze in.

Skin

My rolls are still warm. The coffee's hot. I take the Herald Tribune out from under my tray and put it on the other side of my dishes. The front-page photos are like a bugle's call but no one here pays attention.

Slowly people leave. I get some elbowroom and new companions at the table. My Danish tastes delicious. Everyone looks so happy.

A young woman sits next to me. She starts to talk. She is a college student from some other big city in Denmark. Her summer job just ended and school begins next week. She has one week for vacation and is excited about being in Copenhagen. It is her nation's capital.

She notices my newspaper. She says to me, "Denmark is not threatened by what is happening in Czechoslovakia. We are a member of NATO. America will drop a nuclear bomb on any army that invades us."

She was so sure, so confident, and so happy; it was unnerving. Would America drop the bomb on communist troops invading Denmark? What would happen to the Danes who were nearby?

She and her friends are going to visit Tivoli Gardens this morning. This makes me realize I don't know anything about tourist attractions here. Copenhagen was a city I never planned to visit and it turns out to be the only city I visited twice.

262

I need to get to Paris but if I get an early train today, I will arrive there tonight. That would mean I would have to find a place to sleep and I do not have a Paris hotel in my budget.

If I take the train tonight, I can sleep on the train and be in Paris tomorrow morning. I can spend the day today in Copenhagen. That sounds like a good idea.

I tell her I walked past the entrance to Tivoli Gardens last week. She says it has fields of pretty flowers, amusement rides, music, and places to eat. However, the admission price is more than I can afford.

I ask about other things to see. She mentions art museums but I have seen many art museums. She recommends the palace but I saw palaces in Florence, Rome, Venice, and Vienna.

"You could go shopping," she says.

"I could go shopping?" I am not teasing her. I tell her I am flying home tomorrow and would like to do something different today. I think we are both laughing at this exchange.

She suggests a tour of the Kronenbourg brewery. It is very big, was just built, and has all the newest technology for making beer.

I like the idea. I have never been to where they brew beer. I might learn something.

Then she adds, "And they give you free beer at the end of the tour."

Sold.

Two seconds later she gets up and is gone.

An American takes her place. We introduce ourselves. Right away, he has to tell me he is an American. He looks at the photographs in the Herald Tribune. He is upset. He is worried people will be distracted from the war in Vietnam. I ask if he is against the war.

He wants America to win the war. He brings up the "Domino Effect." He tells me, "I have heard people say the communists will take over every country in Asia and even Australia if we lose in Vietnam."

I tell him, "I believe people who say the Vietnamese are no threat to America or the world. The United States will still be a great country, even after we lose the war."

He ignores what I said. He goes on the offensive. "President Johnson should nuke Vietnam." According to him, that is the quick way to end the war. This young man has nothing but contempt for the anti-war movement. They have prolonged the war. If LBJ would just unleash the military might of the USA against the Vietnamese the war would be over. He wants the war over even if it means dropping the H Bomb.

1968 and I'm Hitchhiking Through Europe

According to me, Americans murdering millions of Vietnamese men, women, and children in an atomic firestorm would be as bad as the Nazis murdering millions of Jews, gypsies, Germans, and others in the holocaust. Maybe Lyndon Baines Johnson does not want to go down in history as the biggest Mass Murderer since Adolph Hitler. Or invite a nuclear response from the U.S.S.R.

I point to some young men speaking German at the table. "25 years ago those men would have been trying to kill us but now Germans and Americans are friends. 25 years from now Vietnamese and Americans will be friends, but more war means fewer of us will be around to be friends."

Again, he ignores my argument. "Are you some kind of pacifist?" he asks me, "Or some kind of coward?"

I get in fights like this all the time back home. I am ready. I know cowards lack courage. Anyone can pull a trigger or push a button that drops a bomb.

"There is a time for war and a time for peace. Germany and Japan had to be defeated for freedom to survive. That war was worth fighting."

Me and most boys my age grew up in awe of the men who beat Fascism and won World War 2. We loved war movies and TV shows with names like *Combat* and *Victory at Sea*. We grew up loving America and wanting to fight for our country. It stood for truth, justice, freedom, and the defeat of tyranny. But with this war, our leaders are lying to us. Politicians will do that.

I am steaming. The war has squandered my generation's patriotism. "I'll fight to overthrow tyrants not help them put down a revolution by their own people."

Americans are not fighting for the Vietnamese people. We do not respect the ordinary person over there. They're called "Gooks." Their farmers are shot at indiscriminately from helicopters; we burn their villages and bomb their towns from the air. Our troops have turned many of their daughters into prostitutes and sons into corpses. Almost a million South Vietnamese have been killed in the war and over 30,000 Americans have died to keep South Vietnam under the thumb of a dictator.

Everybody who studies Vietnam understands the Vietnamese would vote to make their country free of Americans, and free of American bombs. "This war is about defeating the poor Vietnamese people. But if they win, America loses nothing. You tell me why I should fight-kill-die for a dictator! Stop the war!"

I got loud. He has nothing to say. For a second time I ask him to tell me why but he keeps his mouth shut. I hope he will think about it.

I tell him there will be hell to pay if the United States of America stops being a peace-loving nation.

I am someone who follows orders poorly. I ask questions. I stand up for my convictions. I tell him I argue about almost everything with my father but my father has never fought with me about opposing the war or resisting the draft.

The American's face becomes twisted. He shocks me with, "My father died when he was in the army. I don't want to die in Vietnam!"

Now I don't know whether to sympathize with him or to argue him onto the anti-war side. The anti-war movement is a powerful force. We changed the minds of millions of Americans and they voted for anti-war candidates last spring. Our constant opposition was one reason President Johnson did not run for re-election. Our protests completely neutralized pro-war voices demanding America commit mass murder of Vietnamese to keep them "free." Soon we will be able to stop the war. If we stick together, we can change the world.

He changes the subject. He begins to complain about having a miserable vacation. People are treating him like an ugly American. He has not talked to a single European student or seen one interesting thing during his whole trip.

I feel a need to share my secret. It might be

good for this guy to hear it. I tell him about the window and the naked women. He does not believe my story, not one word of it. He wants to go see.

We walk outside together. He takes three steps and looks up. The window is in the shade now. It is totally opaque. He's yelling, accusing me of tricking him. I am saying nothing. I should not have shared what I saw with him anyway. I am happy he does not believe it. I don't care if anyone believes me, ever. It does not change the beauty I had the pleasure of seeing.

The women in the window sure made me feel different. Today is another sunny day. I will go out and see Copenhagen. This has to be a better city than what I saw on my last visit. And I will go to that brewery.

I leave the hostel and take a bus to the railroad station. The overnight train to Paris leaves around 4 P.M. and I buy the cheapest ticket. I have enough money left for meals and some souvenirs. Those I will get in Paris. I have always planned to buy gifts for my parents at the end of the trip so I would not have to carry extra things all over Europe.

It feels good to leave my backpack and bedroll with the station agent. I can walk better. I stop and have lunch.

Soon I am standing outside the Kronenbourg

brewery in a long line with hundreds of other people. We are all waiting for the free tour and free beer.

Inside, I am impressed. It is not at all like the factory I worked in. Everything is shining. All the floors are polished. The metal is all bright steel. Every worker wears a clean white lab coat. I go on a guided tour that includes everything from the boiling hot fermentation tanks to the bottling plant. That bottling plant is a place of total action and extreme noise. I love it.

Some other young people and I are joking, "When do we get to the good part, the free beer." Soon, we arrive at the indoor beer garden. The place is already half filled with a hundred other visitors and they are all sitting at tables on the right side of the room. Our big group comes in, occupies the left side, and they serve us big, half-liter steins of delicious beer. It tastes very good.

It is as if I have not had beer for weeks. I am thirsty and drink it down. Others around me do too. We are all drinking.

The staff is holding singing contests between the group on the right and our group on the left. We are all singing whether we know the words or not. Our side wins on volume alone. This is a great tour.

The right half is leaving. The amicable waitresses are bringing out more steins of

Kronenbourg beer on big trays. Another group is coming in and getting seated in the right half. Lots of us are getting a second half-liter, including me. Another singing contest happens.

This beer is freshly brewed; the best beer I have ever tasted. Everyone around me seems to be having a great time. I am on the greatest tour I could ever imagine. And I'm here just because someone struck up a conversation with me a couple hours ago.

Tour's over?! They are making us stand up to go and I have not even finished my second stein.

"Oh, well."

They are bringing in the next tour group as they are taking our group out. "What's better than more of a good thing?" The idea pops into my head. I simply slip out of the line leaving and into the line entering. I have squeezed myself among a group of college students and am heading back into the beer garden whether it is a good idea or not.

The students missed nothing. Two guys are poking me, laughing and talking to me in German then English. These interactions are happening as we are all walking in and sitting down together at one table. The group is high-spirited. I can tell they are impressed with my daring, maybe. For sure, I know I have a buzz going on in my head.

I ask and they tell me; the two guys are

German college students and the three girls are Danish college students. They met last year during an exchange program and now they are all together again.

I'm happy. I'm saying, "That's great; I'm a college student too."

One of them questions me loudly. He asks, "What are you doing here?"

I lean forward to tell them all. The beer hall is noisy. They all lean forward.

I tell them about hitchhiking back from central Sweden and leaving for Paris by train later today to catch a plane home tomorrow. Then, I throw in I hitchhiked around Europe all summer by myself. They lean back.

The beer arrives. I loudly propose a toast: "Here's to the LIFE OF STUDENTS," while I'm thinking "What-the-hell has gotten into me?" But the toast is a hit! The six of us bang our steins together and drink.

They want to know if I visited Germany.

I tell them Hamburg, Hanover, Nuremburg, Munich, and I flew into Berlin.

They flew into Berlin too. They loved it. I loved it. We toast the citizens of West Berlin.

We're drinking; we're talking. They confirm that I did sleep on a highway deep in the Black Forest. They are definitely impressed with that story.

Their big trip this summer is to this brewery.

The tour is famous with all German students. And FREE BEER. We toast free beer.

They warn me the alcohol content is much higher than American beer. I noticed. I am light headed already. This beer is good but one of them suggests that I should not have a second (fourth) half liter. (One liter = one quart.)

"OK, but I will finish this beer."

I bang the stein on the table and fill my mouth with beer. BAD MOVE!

Freshly brewed beer bubbles up on impact. I do not expect it. My cheeks swell up. I don't know what is happening but I have to lean my head back. Instantly I turn into a VOLCANO of suds. They explode out my mouth, all over me and onto the two students opposite me.

I am terrified. I have spit on two German men.

They laugh. It is beer foam. It's OK.

We are singing. Who is paying attention to the time? Not I.

They ask me what time my train is.

I look; it's one hour from now. Wow. "Can I make it in time?"

They confer. Someone will have to leave with me and take me to the train station. They do not trust I can get there myself. The third girl volunteers and I am delighted for the company. I tell them they have been so good to me today I will never forget them, and everything will work out fine.

The two of us leave quickly. The outside air is refreshing. It helps me turn into a wide-awake drunk and I can walk without a problem. The bus into town is right there. Just a few minutes have gone by since we left the brewery and now we are on our way to central Copenhagen.

But the bus travels slowly. It stops every few blocks; people get on and people get off. My watch is fast. The anxiety is growing. I am tongue-tied with my companion. She is sweet. She is from Copenhagen and points out places she knows.

I am so impressed with how well all these European students I met speak English and I tell her. She is another European who knows they get a very good education in their schools.

We get to the station. It is hit or miss now. We run in and head to the station agent for my gear. She warns me maybe they just announced all aboard for the Paris train. I don't know because it's all in Danish. She can't tell for sure because the announcer sounds like he is underwater.

She excuses herself and me to everyone in line as we jump to the front to get my backpack and bedroll. This is not fast. And that was the last boarding call.

Another minute goes by. Everyone is looking at us. Employees are still searching for my stuff.

I tell her to forget about my bags. "I can't miss this train." I am ready to run for it.

She says, "Don't leave your bags."

Finally my bags are found, too late. I could be in a worse place. I have a friend. She is not upset. She says I can catch the next train to Paris. She will find out when it leaves and what time it arrives. I start thinking about what time my plane takes off.

We go to the ticket window to exchange tickets. She shows them my ticket and does all the talking. She talks to them for a long time.

Finally, she turns around and tells me a train is leaving in 45 minutes that will stop in Hamburg tonight while the Paris train is still in the Hamburg train station. I can transfer to the same Paris train I missed here, in Hamburg.

I say something like "Let me get this straight, the new train catches up to the old train in 45 minutes and the Hamburg train leaves for Paris."

This may have confused her. She tells me I do not want the train to Hamburg. That is just one of its stops. She consults again with the man in the window. We do not even have to exchange my ticket.

The next thing I know she asks, "What would you like to do for the next 45 minutes."

I am thrilled she will stay with me until my train leaves and I tell her. She knows I'm drunk. I know I'm drunk. Missing the train and watching her ask questions in Danish convinced me I would be absolutely lost right now.

I tell her I am not sure I could have made it by myself. "Are you my Guardian Angel?"

She understands that. She laughs.

I suggest we get something to eat.

The restaurant in the station has tables next to the tracks. We sit down. We both check the restaurant clock. It says 4:45. The train leaves at 5:15, plenty of time.

She is not hungry and orders a Kronenbourg beer. I am hungry and order a sandwich, potatoes, and a glass of water. I pay when served. Food is good. Talk is better. I tell her about my life at school and the great big old house my friends and I live in.

She tells me European students are visiting each other's countries all the time. Today, students feel more European than Danish, German, or French so there will never be another war in Europe.

"Why would one European nation invade another European nation?" she says. "World War 2 was the last war in Europe."

She loves Denmark. It is a great country and America is a great country like Denmark. She is glad we are in NATO together because it makes the world a safer place.

Time flies, but the clock stands still. She notices it first. The hands of the clock are still at 4:45. I can't believe it! The clock in the station restaurant shouldn't be broken but IT IS BROKEN! My watch says 5:15 exactly!

We both start running, carrying my stuff. There is a train still on the right track but no one is on the platform except a conductor. There by one minute; no the train starts moving very slowly. The conductor motions at us to get on but only I am leaving.

She kisses me. We kiss again. Quickly, she is trying to get something from the conductor. He gives her a pen and paper. We are walking along as the train moves faster. I get the pen and paper. I write down my name. The train is speeding up. The conductor is jumping on. He is demanding something in Danish. She's saying, "Jump on now or he will shut the door." I jump.

It is the kind of door where he can shut the bottom half and the top half stays open. She and I talk across the top half. She's walking quickly next to us. The train noise increases. I am yelling now, "I live in a great big city. Come visit our commune. Bring your friends. People crash in our living room all the time. I would love to see you again."

Now she is running next to the door shouting at the conductor in Danish. I hear her saying the words "Hamburg," and "Paris." This young woman really is my Guardian Angel.

As loudly I as can, I yell "Thank you." The conductor pulls me back. My hand sticks out. It waves goodbye.

My head is swimming. My stomach is rock steady. The train's motion feels good. I made it by the skin of my teeth and promise myself I will not do that again. If I had five minutes to spare I would now have a beautiful friend in Copenhagen to write to and maybe see again.

The conductor and I look out at the city as the train speeds up on the tracks. He adjusts his pen. He is a young man. I sense embarrassment from him. I hope he has, or will have someone who kisses him with passion.

He does speak English. He says Hamburg and my connection for the train to Paris is eight hours away. He will not be the conductor then. His shift ends when this train rolls into a large ferry. I know about the ferry between Denmark and Germany.

The Danish conductor promises to ask the officer on the ferry to tell the German conductor to make sure I transfer to the Paris train when this train gets to Hamburg.

We are still in the noisy vestibule between the cars. Our train is moving fast. I will go sit down in a minute or two. I look at Copenhagen out the open door and the conductor looks too, and he watches me. The wind refreshes our faces.

Well, my adventure is over. There is nothing to a train ride. In 24 hours, I will be in an airplane flying home. I promised myself I would write down some memories. The next thing I am going to do is find a seat and start writing.

CHAPTER 12

THE FAR OUT

Inside the train, I see the unexpected. Instead of bench seats, there is a long hallway lined with windows on the right side and private compartments on the left, and all the doors are open. I've seen this in the movies.

A big family occupies the first compartment. I move on.

A group of older men smoking cigarettes is inside the second. I look at them; they look me over, up and down. I think about going in but shuffle past them with my backpack and bedroll and move on down the hallway.

The third contains students, bags and suitcases but there is a seat. I ask if I can join them.

One says yes. Two ignore me and two just stare. One stare turns into a dirty look.

I am thinking, "I'm allowed to sit here" so I flip my stuff onto the rack above the seats and sit next to the person who welcomed me. She is a small blond woman about my age. And she smiles at me.

She volunteers they are American students who have been touring Europe for three weeks. She is speaking quietly. I can barely hear her over noise from the train. Tonight they are going to Frankfurt and tomorrow taking the plane home. I tell her I am also a college student but going to Paris. I too will be taking the plane home tomorrow.

No one else is talking. The rhythm of the train is what I am hearing. A minute goes by in silence. She asks, in a soft voice, "Does this train go to Paris?"

I tell her about transferring to the Paris train when we get to Hamburg. I close my eyes. I have found another good spot. Another minute goes by.

I try to restart conversation with her and ask if she has enjoyed her trip. She starts to answer but she is interrupted.

"What are you doing here?" someone is asking me. The voice is loud and demanding.

The woman who gave me the dirty look asked that question. She is the tallest of the group, a brunette whose short curly hair looks very good on her. But I would never compliment her now. I ignore her rude tone. I answer her question.

I give her the same answer I gave the Germans at the Kronenbourg brewery about hitchhiking back from central Sweden, taking the train to Paris, and catching the plane home tomorrow.

Now she is asking why I was hitchhiking back from Sweden but Ice, Bent, and almost going to jail in Jonkoping is a story I am not telling.

Instead, speaking up so everyone can hear me I say, "I hitchhiked through Europe for the summer and got as far north as Sweden before I had to turn around to come home." And I add, with relief and satisfaction "My trip was great, really, really great."

The brunette challenges me. She says, "Great? What makes that so great?"

The two girls who ignored me giggle.

"I learned a lot."

"Oh yeah sure, like what?"

"All summer I kept on running into Europeans whose lives are like the lives of my parents, my aunts and uncles, teachers I know, waitresses, and even police. The people I met may all live in Europe but they were not foreigners."

"You learned that how?"

These weren't questions. They were put-downs.

"People opened their doors for me; we drove for

hours together." I tell them how Europeans took me into their homes where I met their families; we shared meals together and some even put me up for the night.

The fifth woman in the group, sitting next to the brunette blurts out, "He had the kind of trip I wanted to have!"

I add, "I just talked to a lot of Europeans this summer and learned from them."

The small girl next to me sticks this to the brunette: "You said we would talk to Europeans. We only talked to American tourists this whole trip."

Someone defends her, "We talked to those boys in Italy!"

More of the group starts to complain.

"I didn't get to speak any French at all."

"We never stopped traveling around!"

Volume goes up. Everyone is talking.

"Those weren't boys!"

"You promised us a lot of fun!"

Someone throws a question at me asking if I had any trouble with the police. I do not get a chance to answer.

Two girls are upset and loud; their parents paid a lot for this vacation and they could have had more fun at home.

The brunette is the leader and she is being hit with more complaints. Now she's raising her voice and telling them how her father helped everybody go first class. And about how they told him they wanted the best trip money could buy and he had delivered.

I am quiet. I know money can't buy everything, never true friendship. These five young women have been together too long. They went from everyone being quiet to everyone yelling at one another in seconds. There is no more giggling. Action happens.

The woman sitting next to the brunette punches her in the shoulder. "WHAP" is the sound it makes. I am shocked. I could tell it hurt. Maybe it hurt her ego more than her shoulder but it hurt.

"Stop!" the brunette yells, but the other girl hits her again.

The leader grabs the other girl's hands. There is no struggle. The girl who did the punching just stops. But she is really pissed off. "I am sick and tired of hearing about your father and your trip." She goes on about the brunette taking charge of the trip somehow and stopping them from doing anything fun. She is fed up with looking at old stuff in art museums and old museums, museums and ruins, museums and churches.

I saw great art, fabulous, beautiful and sometimes funny art, and I will probably forget most of it. But I will never forget many, many of the people who touched my life while I was hitchhiking.

All this talk and action is happening and only one minute ago it was quiet. Now the hitting changes things.

The girls lower their volume; they are still upset. I hear more complaints about how they didn't have any fun.

The brunette's one solid defender among the girls tells them all, "None of us ever got sick."

"We ate at hotels. Every meal was at a hotel," someone replies. They agree no one has any complaints about the hotels or the food.

The blonde next to me says she is still glad she came on the trip. The girl who punched the brunette stands up and changes sides. She squeezes in on our bench. Now four people face two.

Complaining ceases. Talking dies. No one is offering the brunette an apology. It becomes very quiet.

I have been sitting in this compartment for only a few minutes and I have started an argument. But maybe I just witnessed a fight going on and off for weeks now.

It isn't a good. I am not feeling good about being with these women and this compartment.

One girl, a giggler who was the brunette's sole defender gets up and pushes through us to leave. She gives me a dirty look as she goes out the door.

1968 and I'm Hitchhiking Through Europe

The return of silence focuses my hearing on the rhythmical sound of the train going down the tracks.

I begin thinking how some people bring along their problems when they travel. And about the trouble they cause other people. Have I been like that? I do not want to go where those thoughts will take me.

I break the silence by asking the blonde if she ever saw any slums in Europe. During my trip, I asked other Americans about this and people said they never saw any slums. I tell her about walking around in every city I visited and never seeing bad housing like in the U.S.

I tell her, at my university I live near block after block of beaten-up old rowhouses with bad plumbing, broken windows, rotting porches, and peeling paint. Poor families and college students live in places unfit for human habitation. Every month they pay rent to some scumbag landlord for the privilege of living in his pisshole.

Again, I have said one of those things I want to take back. By the look on her face, I know I have turned her off. Maybe it was showing my anger about something peculiar to the United States and Third world countries. Maybe her dad is a scumbag.

She tells me they did not take that kind of trip.

The brunette tells us to shut up; she has a headache. Now no one is talking again.

Except the conductor, who appears in the doorway with the girl who left. He is the conductor I know. "Excuse me young man," he says, "May I see your ticket."

High anxiety hits me in my stomach. Did I get the ticket back from my Danish friend? It's not in my pants pockets. I pull my backpack off the shelf. It is not in the outside pocket there either. I am starting to sweat when I find my ticket tucked inside my jacket under the backpack's flap.

The conductor looks at it and says, "This compartment is in the first class section and your ticket is for second class." He tells me I have to move two cars forward.

I actually feel relieved. I turn and retrieve my bedroll but I do not look at the brunette, the gigglers, or the girl who did the punching. I do not want to see the smirks or smiles they may have on their faces. I am happy to get out of here.

I do say to the blonde girl. "I will be just two cars away if you would like to come back and talk with me later." Fat chance of that happening.

"OK," she says along with "goodbye."

The brunette says something like "fat chance."

In the corridor, the conductor tells me he always knew I did not pay for a seat in the first class compartments. He decided to let me sit there anyway because he thought I would be good for the students. He only took me out because of the complaint. If he had his way, I would still be sitting there.

"It's OK."

Second class has regular train seats. It is not crowded and I sit by myself.

My backpack will be my writing surface. I pull it up onto my lap and dig out my pen and notepad. I will start by drawing a map of my journey. I draw an "S" shape and put in some names of cities I visited but my head goes down onto the backpack. My eyes close. I fall fast asleep.

I sleep the rest of the way through Denmark. No one wakes me up to tell me to go upstairs when the train gets loaded into the big ferry and crosses the sea to Germany so I sleep through that too. I sleep through the changing of conductors and the train ride through Northern Germany.

Someone pokes me awake in a rush. I sense the train is not moving.

"Hurry hurry Paris train hurry run." A conductor is standing over me and TAKING MY STUFF. I am hardly awake, mostly asleep; everybody in the train car is looking at me and I have to go to the bathroom.

He's yelling now in German and I'm jerking myself up. I am following him, really running down the aisle. He is carrying my backpack and bedroll. We are out onto the platform. I am still half-asleep and have ABSOLUTELY NO IDEA WHAT TRACK THE PARIS TRAIN IS ON. Hurry, hurry, where?

Two conductors are standing alongside another train on the opposite side of this platform. They are just five or six meters away and are waving at me. That must be the train to Paris. I run over to it.

One of the conductors greets me with, "You are lucky you made it."

The other says, "The German conductor had to search the entire train. You are lucky he found you."

"Yes, I am lucky." But I made this train to Paris because of the feelings between my Danish friend and I, and the impression she made on the conductor in Copenhagen, and the story he told to the officer on the ferry. And also because of how much the new conductor in Germany remembered, and his willingness to search the train to find the sleeping young American hitchhiker. Yes, it was part luck, and it was part humanity.

I board the train and go in the bathroom. A big sign in many languages says, "Don't use these toilets while the train is in the station." They flush directly onto the tracks. This stops me only for about one second. Anyway, by the time I flush we are moving full speed to Paris.

It is probably the middle of the night. I walk into an empty train car, lie down on a seat, and fall fast asleep. No one wakes me up again.

I open my eyes to the daytime as the train sits in a station somewhere. My train car is empty. I look out onto a brown concrete platform in a huge train shed covered by a dirty glass roof. Not a soul is in sight. I am in some big city and I walk to the train's door with hesitation. Where am I?

Even outside the train, I am not sure this is Paris. I have no idea if my train has been sitting here for an hour or if it will pull out in one minute to finish the trip. And there is no one to ask.

Looking around, I begin thinking this is not 1968. Old, torn posters with faded colors advertise products from the 50's. Decades of dirt coat the orange brick walls. Several locomotives at the railheads are from when both steam and diesel engines pulled the trains. The place smells of oil. Light filters through the dirty glass roof and diffuses all around creating no shadows. The station could be in some old black and white movie from the 1930's. I loved those movies.

This is Paris; I can feel it.

Straight ahead is the main concourse. There are train tracks and a large, black, steam locomotive sitting right next to tables of a French café. I see some very well dressed people having coffee and reading the papers.

Walking forward, I mix with the Parisians. And I am aware of something, I'm no longer intimidated here, or self-conscious when they look at me.

I will join them for breakfast. I buy a croissant, a cup of espresso, and a cut-up apple. I pay with an American dollar. The strong coffee is delicious. I get a second cup.

I realize how low my funds are and change my last few dollars into French francs. These will have to buy lunch, gifts for my parents, and a ticket for the bus to the airport.

American money for the NYC airport is not necessary because a friend is meeting us there and taking us home. I can spend all my money in Paris but I must buy that bus ticket first.

I check the schedule and buy a ticket for the bus that gets to the airport an hour before my plane departs. I will remember I need to catch the 3:30 bus.

I promise myself no more high anxiety moments. I set my watch correctly. I say aloud, "I will pay attention to the time."

I can spend the next few hours wandering around Paris. I check my map and go outside. My last day in Europe is another beautiful day.

I do not want to pay subway fare. I just start

walking in the direction of the Notre Dame Cathedral. It is something to see and a place to sit down.

The Notre Dame has been a cathedral for eight centuries. Many people famous in their time are buried under stone slabs on the floor. I can hear, see, and smell history here. I am more impressed by this place than Saint Peter's in the Vatican.

Any pew of a medieval cathedral is a good place to rest. I observe people's styles and rituals. I can pick out the tourists. I see other people who look like regular parishioners. Imagine your church is the ancient, giant Notre Dame Cathedral in Paris.

Why are these people crawling up the aisles on their knees? They must be on a pilgrimage asking God for something special.

I will never get tired of observation and interpretation.

I walk along the Seine. The river has boat traffic on it, tourist, commercial, industrial, and residential. Dogs run around on top of moving barges and every moored houseboat.

So many people are walking around Paris some streets become sidewalks. Cars stop. Pedestrians rule. There are even more people out today than I saw on the streets of crowded West Berlin.

I meander through Paris' cobblestone streets. Trees, shops, and people are a visual constant. The orientation of streets and the absence of high-rise buildings allow the sun to brighten my walk.

A bridge draws me to the south side of the river Seine; the area is called the Left Bank. Crowds are here too.

As I walk around, the cobblestone streets remind me of Barbara and the rock her husband pumped up and down the night I met him. There is no hint of the violent fighting that occurred on these streets just a few months ago.

On the left bank along the river, I see a man waving two swords over his head and shouting. I hope he is promising everyone a show.

Many people are curious enough to stop walking by. He quickly attracts a crowd. His audience forms a densely packed circle ten meters in diameter. This is a big circle and he maintains his open space by running around waving his swords and scaring everyone. He means business. Nobody is going to get too close. I am in the back of the crowd, glad to be tall.

He is thin and wearing black pants. His chest is bare. This man's torso has no fat. Tattoos, scars, muscles and ribs pop off him and into my eyes. Swords, daggers, and other things lie at his feet.

He stops running. Now he is yelling. I do not understand his words but his shrill tone keeps everyone's attention.

The man stands in the circle's center and his performance begins.

At the circus long ago, I saw a man juggle one, two, three swords. It inspires awe.

Our street performer juggles swords well. And while he is juggling he runs in his circle, again keeping the crowd at bay. A few people (I) give him some applause.

I never really saw someone swallow a sword. On TV, yes but in real life, from a short distance away no. Our street performer picks up a two-edged sword with a narrow pointed blade. It looks longer than his torso and he has a hard time swallowing it.

With his jerking movements and guttural noises, he is exciting the crowd. With the final few inches of penetration when he begins gagging, the crowd begins to breathe faster. He leans back and completes swallowing the entire blade.

He pulls out the sword slowly and looks at us. A few more people give him some applause. He is not finished.

Next, he takes a sword in each hand.

The sword swallower is running in his circle waving the swords around, yelling and now spinning like a whirling dervish. I am feeling some threat but most of the crowd is holding its position. Just a few people are deserting the front ranks.

He swallows two swords at the same time. I have never even heard of this and he gets more applause. He pulls out the swords and screams at us but I do not understand. People buzz. The applause increases as he runs his circle again and waves his swords.

I don't need to understand French to enjoy the show. I am actually impressed with something unexpected and very memorable. I am watching a real street performance by a very crazy guy.

A few people walk forward and put money in a box. The show might be over but the performer is not packing up his gear. Maybe he will swallow three swords or return to juggling; he doesn't.

He starts again, quietly this time. In an exaggerated motion, he points to the ground at a short dagger with a jeweled handle and picks it up.

The dagger is only as long as the distance from your wrist to your fingertips. Its blade is as thin as an ice pick. Compared to his swords, it does not impress. I have no clue about what he is going do with the dagger.

The man jabs it, hard, into a piece of wood. It sticks up. He runs around the edge of the circle showing everyone what he has. He pries it out and places it next to his bicep. He says nothing.

Slowly, very slowly he is pushing the dagger

into a dark spot on his upper arm. Turning around, he shows this to everyone. It is amazing! The blade is disappearing between his bicep and the bone. There is no blood!

The buzz from the crowd is strong. There is an even greater reaction when first the point, then the blade, appears on the other side of his arm. People gasp; many applaud, a few cheer.

How can this be? It can't be a trick because his bare arm has part of the blade on each side. Where is the blood?

The performer smiles for the first time and I notice his gold front teeth.

He takes his hand off the dagger and slowly rotates so everyone can get a good look. We all see a dagger sticking through this man's bare arm, hanging in his muscle. And he sees each one of us, our eyes fixed on him.

He is getting more applause now. He does not run in a circle. He yells. He slowly pulls out the dagger and holds it against his neck.

He leans his head back and begins pushing it down into his neck, below his Adam's apple. He is turning around 360 degrees. He finishes. His arms are hanging down, stiff and his open hands turn outwards.

Now he is turning around and putting himself

on display with no bleeding that shows, just a dagger in his throat, through the skin. Some people are applauding, others cheering, but most are just standing quietly.

The show is over.

Without drama, he twists out the dagger. But he is not done.

With the serious, strong voice of a great showman, he tells the crowd something. He runs the perimeter of the circle, a street performer, his dagger, and his bare chest pushed out.

He looks down. He touches the dagger's tip to a dark, raised, scarred circle of flesh on his chest. He works the point into that spot. It is between some ribs, near his heart. He eases it in slowly, and he stops. The man speaks to the crowd. We are very silent. You could hear a pin drop.

Immediately, it changes. He is yelling, then comes up to the edge of his audience. He walks around his circle, leaning back, holding the dagger, and looking directly at individuals in the audience. The dagger is sticking straight up from his chest.

Everyone backs up. Some take several steps back. There is more applause. He pulls out the dagger and bows. He smiles. Show's over.

I have been stunned. I keep backing up as the crowd disperses. He is still yelling. Some people are walking up and giving him money. I can't. I can't get closer. The few francs I have left are for lunch and presents.

I am walking away and hearing another American saying he was disgusted. Yeah, but he stayed to watch. His partner's reply is about pickpockets working the crowd. I touch my wallet.

After several hours of walking, sitting, and watching, I am now eating a late lunch on a beautiful day in Paris. The food from a vendor on a Parisian street is good and cheap.

I walk all the way over to the Eiffel Tower. There are long lines of people waiting to take the elevator up to the top. I don't have the time.

I buy mom a small model of the tower. It is only four inches tall but heavy like a paperweight. She will like it and it costs a couple francs, about forty cents. I have francs left over but have no idea what to buy my father.

A small café lures me over and I sit down at a sidewalk table with its view of the Eiffel Tower. Over the doorway low prices are posted on a sign. Coffee is just two francs.

The waiter is a nice young man who speaks English like an American. I look at the time. I have twenty minutes before I have to begin my trip back to catch the bus. I sit down.

I lean back. This café is so like all of Europe to me. This is my Europe like Philadelphia is my city.

Next summer I will travel around the United States. I want to get to know it as my country. I have never seen the Rocky Mountains, been to New Orleans or San Francisco. I know I live in a beautiful country. I would love to see all of America. Maybe I will hitchhike; maybe I will go with a friend, buy an old jalopy and pick up hitchhikers.

I miss our house. I hope the university didn't speed-up the demolition schedule and knock it down while I was away.

This summer I know I missed a lot back home. My friends went to demonstrations against the war. They are organizing another big one for the fall. I sent them one postcard. I must get back.

The sunshine feels as wonderful as it has so many other days during the last two months. I ask myself, "Did I have an adventure this summer? Am I more the man I want to be?" My memories, the nice breeze, a great cup of coffee, and seeing the Eiffel Tower and all these good people in the park make me very content with my answers to these questions.

Then the waiter delivers the check.

It is many times what the posted sign said the coffee would cost.

I look at my watch. My time is up.

In an instant, all my calm disappears.

I go off at the waiter, "I don't want to be ripped off!" I am loud enough to be drawing the stares of all the other patrons seated outside. "This check is too much!"

I point out how the coffee is supposed to be two francs but he isn't looking at any sign. I'm scared too because the check is for more money than I have left. "I don't have enough francs to pay this!"

There is an inside price and an outside price. The waiter defends the check as normal when you sit outside and look at the tower.

He asks if I am just beginning my visit to France. He says he will take U.S. dollars instead of francs.

At a much lower volume I tell him today is the last day of a summer of hitchhiking. He and I go on talking.

"Then you should know about higher prices outdoors."

"I do, but I still don't want to be ripped off. When the sign says one price and the check says another, it is a rip off!"

"What sign?" he is demanding at the same time I am telling him I don't have any American dollars left either.

Again, I am pointing above the door to the

prices on the sign and he is looking there as if he doesn't see anything.

I pull all the francs and smaller coins I have out of my pockets and put them on the table.

Somehow, for some reason probably unknown even to the waiter he changes his tone. He stops being defensive and talks to me normally. And I calm down. Embarrassment sets in.

"I hope your hitchhiking around Europe was not filled with being ripped off," he says.

"It wasn't. People were wonderful to me. Today my thoughts are filled with good memories. I just don't want to be ripped off on the last day of my trip."

Now he is telling me, "You didn't read the sign right."

I am not agreeing with him but there is fine print at the bottom; they are indoor prices.

Now he is looking at the coins on the table and saying, "I'm sorry you didn't understand the prices, pay me what you can."

I take back a couple francs for the subway. I take back a couple of francs to get my stuff from where I checked it. And I tell him what those coins are for. I leave him the rest and thank him for understanding. I have to run.

I get to the entrance to the Paris Metro. Down on the platform I wait a long time while nothing happens. My anxiety level is overwhelming me now. The metro takes days to arrive.

I see hours click off on my watch during the ride. We stop at every station. We seem to wait longer and longer at every stop. The time is getting closer and closer to 3:30. Very soon I will have to be at the place to catch the bus. When the train gets to my stop, it is only 3:15 but I run up those stairs.

First, I have to pick up my stuff. I'm glad there is no line. After I pay, I realize I have only one franc to my name, about twenty cents.

Where is my bus ticket? A quick body search finds it in the last place I look. Now I have to find where to catch the bus to the airport.

Someone who looks like he works at the train station walks by; maybe he can help me. I ask him, "Where is the bus to the airport?" But I don't speak his language.

There are no signs saying "Bus to the airport." But how would I know? I can't read French either. It is now 3:25 P.M.

"Oh, why didn't I learn some French in school?"

I go outside looking. The sign says Autobus Aeroport. This must be the place. There is a crowd of people waiting, Americans. They confirm this is where you wait for the airport bus. And wait, and wait.

There was no 3 PM bus. People are complaining about that. I hear someone say they have been waiting here since 2:30. There might be more of us than the bus can carry. Everyone is worried about catching their plane.

It is after 3:30 now, and no bus in sight. I worry too.

The bus arrives. We all crowd on-board. I am standing in the aisle. I am not the only one standing. The bus pulls out and we are swaying back and forth.

"I will make it; I will make it." I am saying this aloud.

An American couple wants to help me. They are my parent's age. One asks what time my plane is.

I tell them, "One hour and twenty minutes from now."

A traffic jam catches our bus. I feel it begin to stop and go, stop and go, very slowly. We started the trip late and will arrive late.

The woman asks if I am due at the airport at five, or if five is the time on the ticket.

Five PM is the ticket time.

"Oh, that's when the plane takes off. They might close the gate a half hour earlier," she says.

He tells me occasionally there is a line to show passports.

My passport! My ticket! I touch the top of the

money belt around my waist. They are right where I kept them all summer.

He says, "Sometimes passengers have to open up their bags for inspection and..." He always tries to get to the airport at least an hour earlier.

They are no help! And I was trying to get there an hour earlier. But the bus was late.

I keep my mouth shut now. We were told the plane leaves at five. It will not leave without me. I will be on the plane. I am still worried.

The bus creeps forward in bumper-to-bumper traffic.

I am waiting for the airport bus to move longer than I waited outside Genoa, Italy. I am sweating more than I did when I spent a broiling day by the German Autobahn. I am more nervous than I was on the bus ride to Ice's house. However, no ride will ever be as scary as my first ride-in the Pyrenees.

Finally we are on a highway. Eventually I see the airport. It is 4:30 but we drive some more. When the bus driver opens the doors, I run.

The big board lists my charter flight to New York City. The plane departs from a nearby gate.

I'm running and my stuff is bouncing. I see Jim. We are waving at one another. He and another friend George are the only people still waiting outside the plane.

They greet me with smiles and curses, yelling, "We worried about having to hold the doors open until you made it!"

I made it.

And they both want to know, right then, "WHERE HAVE YOU BEEN?"

THE END

The future belongs
To those who believe
In the beauty of their dreams

Eleanor Roosevelt

Author's note – the events in this book happened, the people existed, and the conversations are written as I remember them.

Some events are not in chronological order. And, to be completely honest, I should have used the word approximately a hundred times: i.e. approximately twenty-five miles, approximately one month ago, approximately twelve million workers on strike, etc.

All references to beauty and the weather are subjective.

ACKNOWLEDGEMENTS

I acknowledge my great wife of 35 years has always been my saving grace. Her editing skills sharpened the rough edges of this story immeasurably.
Thank you.
My wife and daughters read my first draft and their enthusiasm was the nourishment my soul needed to keep moving ahead.
Thank you.
My son used his creativity and skills in the graphic arts to design the dust jacket and format the text. He did a wonderful job.
Thank you.

To order an additional hardcover copy of
1968 and I'm Hitchhiking Through Europe
By Joe Mack
go to http://www.solidpress.com

All sales taxes are included in the price